The Complete Keto Chaffle Cookbook

Over 160 Delicious And Easy To Prepare Low Carb And High Fat Waffle Recipes

Elena Baker

TABLE OF CONTENTS

RECIPES

Quick & Easy Blueberry Chaffle

Preparation Time: 15 minutes Servings: 2

Ingredients:

- 1 egg, lightly beaten

- 1/4 cup blueberries

- 1/2 tsp vanilla

- 1 oz cream cheese

- 1/4 tsp baking powder, gluten-free

- 4 tsp Swerve

- 1 tbsp coconut flour

Directions:

1. Preheat your waffle maker.

2. In a small bowl, mix coconut flour, baking powder, and Swerve until well combined.

3. Add vanilla, cream cheese, egg, and vanilla and whisk until combined.

4. Spray waffle maker with cooking spray.

5. Pour half batter in the hot waffle maker and top with 4-5 blueberries and cook for 4-5 minutes until golden brown. Repeat with the remaining batter.

6. Serve and enjoy.

Nutrition: Calories 135 Fat 8.2 g Carbohydrates 11 g Sugar 2.6 g Protein 5 g Cholesterol 97 mg

Apple Cinnamon Chaffles

Preparation Time: 20 minutes Servings: 3

Ingredients:

- 3 eggs, lightly beaten

- 1 cup mozzarella cheese, shredded

- ¼ cup apple, chopped

- ½ tsp monk fruit sweetener

- 1 ½ tsp cinnamon

- ¼ tsp baking powder, gluten- free

- 2 tbsp coconut flour

Directions:

1. Preheat your waffle maker.

2. Add eggs in a mixing bowl and beat until frothy.

3. Add remaining ingredients and stir until well combined.

4. Spray waffle maker with cooking spray.

5. Pour 1/3 of batter in the hot waffle maker and cook for 4 minutes or until golden brown. Repeat with the remaining batter.

6. Serve and enjoy.

Nutrition: Calories 142 Fat 7.4 g Carbohydrates 9.7 g Sugar 3 g Protein 9.6 g Cholesterol 169 mg

Mozzarella Peanut Butter Chaffle

Preparation Time: 15 minutes Servings: 2

Ingredients:

- 1 egg, lightly beaten

- 2 tbsp peanut butter

- 2 tbsp Swerve

- 1/2 cup mozzarella cheese, shredded

Directions:

1. Preheat your waffle maker.

2. In a bowl, mix egg, cheese, Swerve, and peanut butter until well combined.

3. Spray waffle maker with cooking spray.

4. Pour half batter in the hot waffle maker and cook for 4 minutes or until golden brown. Repeat with the remaining batter.

5. Serve and enjoy.

Nutrition: Calories 150 Fat 11.5 g
Carbohydrates 5.6 g Sugar 1.7 g
Protein 8.8 g Cholesterol 86 mg

Sweet Vanilla Chocolate Chaffle

Preparation Time: 10 minutes Servings: 1

Ingredients:

- 1 egg, lightly beaten

- 1/4 tsp cinnamon

- 1/2 tsp vanilla

- 1 tbsp Swerve

- 2 tsp unsweetened cocoa powder

- 1 tbsp coconut flour

- 2 oz cream cheese, softened

Directions:

1. Add all ingredients into the small bowl and mix until well combined.

2. Spray waffle maker with cooking spray.

3. Pour batter in the hot waffle maker and cook until golden brown.

4. Serve and enjoy.

Nutrition: Calories 312 Fat 25.4 g
Carbohydrates 11.5 g Sugar 0.8 g
Protein 11.6 g Cholesterol 226 mg

Peanut Butter Sandwich Chaffle

Preparation Time: 15 minutes Servings: 1

Ingredients:

For chaffle:

- 1 egg, lightly beaten

- 1/2 cup mozzarella cheese, shredded

- 1/4 tsp espresso powder

- 1 tbsp unsweetened chocolate chips

- 1 tbsp Swerve

- 2 tbsp unsweetened cocoa powder

For filling:

- 1 tbsp butter, softened

- 2 tbsp Swerve

- 3 tbsp creamy peanut butter

Directions:

1. Preheat your waffle maker.

2. In a bowl, whisk together egg, espresso powder, chocolate chips, Swerve, and cocoa powder.

3. Add mozzarella cheese and stir well.

4. Spray waffle maker with cooking spray.

5. Pour 1/2 of the batter in the hot waffle maker and cook for 3-4 minutes or until golden brown. Repeat with the remaining batter.

For filling:

1. In a small bowl, stir together butter, Swerve, and peanut butter until smooth.

2. Once chaffles is cool, then spread filling mixture between two chaffle and place in the fridge for 10 minutes.

3. Cut chaffle sandwich in half and serve.

Nutrition: Calories 190 Fat 16.1 g
Carbohydrates 9.6 g Sugar 1.1 g
Protein 8.2 g Cholesterol 101 mg

Cherry Chocolate Chaffle

Preparation Time: 10 minutes Servings: 1

Ingredients:

- 1 egg, lightly beaten

- 1 tbsp unsweetened chocolate chips

- 2 tbsp sugar-free cherry pie filling

- 2 tbsp heavy whipping cream

- 1/2 cup mozzarella cheese, shredded

- 1/2 tsp baking powder, gluten-free

- 1 tbsp Swerve

- 1 tbsp unsweetened cocoa powder

- 1 tbsp almond flour

Directions:

1. Preheat the waffle maker.

2. In a bowl, whisk together egg, cheese, baking powder, Swerve, cocoa powder, and almond flour.

3. Spray waffle maker with cooking spray.

4. Pour batter in the hot waffle maker and cook until golden brown.

5. Top with cherry pie filling, heavy whipping cream, and chocolate chips and serve.

Nutrition: Calories 264 Fat 22 g
Carbohydrates 8.5 g Sugar 0.5 g
Protein 12.7 g Cholesterol 212 mg

Pulled Pork Chaffle Sandwiches

Preparation Time: 20 minutes Cooking Time: 28 minutes Servings: 4

Ingredients:

- 2 eggs, beaten

- 1 cup finely grated cheddar cheese
- ¼ tsp baking powder

- 2 cups cooked and shredded pork

- 1 tbsp sugar-free BBQ sauce

- 2 cups shredded coleslaw mix

- 2 tbsp apple cider vinegar

- ½ tsp salt

- ¼ cup ranch dressing

Directions:

1. Preheat the waffle iron.

2. In a medium bowl, mix the eggs, cheddar cheese, and baking powder.

3. Open the iron and add a quarter of the mixture. Close and cook until crispy, 7 minutes.

4. Transfer the chaffle to a plate and make 3 more chaffles in the same manner.

5. Meanwhile, in another medium bowl, mix the pulled pork with the BBQ sauce until well combined. Set aside.

6. Also, mix the coleslaw mix, apple cider vinegar, salt, and ranch dressing in another medium bowl.

7. When the chaffles are ready, on two pieces, divide the pork and then top with the ranch coleslaw. Cover with the remaining chaffles and insert mini skewers to secure the sandwiches.

8. Enjoy afterward.

Nutrition: Calories 374 Fats 23.61g Carbs 8.2g Net Carbs 8.2g Protein 28.05g

Simple Ham Chaffle

Time: 15 minutes Serve: 2

Ingredients:

- 1 egg, lightly beaten

- 1/4 cup ham, chopped
- 1/2 cup cheddar cheese, shredded

- 1/4 tsp garlic salt

For Dip:

- 1 1/2 tsp Dijon mustard

- 1 tbsp mayonnaise

Directions:

1. Preheat your waffle maker.

2. Whisk eggs in a bowl.

3. Stir in ham, cheese, and garlic salt until combine.

4. Spray waffle maker with cooking spray.

5. Pour half of the batter in the hot waffle maker and cook for 3-4 minutes or until

golden brown. Repeat with the remaining batter.

For Dip:

1. In a small bowl, mix mustard and mayonnaise.

2. Serve chaffle with dip.

Nutrition: Calories 205 Fat 15.6 g Carbohydrates 3.4 g Sugar 0.9 g Protein 12.9 g Cholesterol 123 mg

Delicious Bagel Chaffle

Time: 15 minutes Serve: 2

Ingredients:

- 1 egg, lightly beaten

- 1/4 tsp garlic powder

- 1/4 tsp onion powder

- 1 1/2 tsp bagel seasoning

- 3/4 cup mozzarella cheese, shredded

- 1/2 tsp baking powder, gluten-free

- 1 tbsp almond flour

Directions:

1. Preheat your waffle maker.

2. In a bowl, mix egg, bagel seasoning, baking powder, onion powder, garlic powder, and almond flour until well combined.

3. Add cheese and stir well.

4. Spray waffle maker with cooking spray.

5. Pour 1/2 of batter in the hot waffle maker and cook for 5 minutes or until golden brown. Repeat with the remaining batter.

6. Serve and enjoy.

Nutrition: Calories 85 Fat 5.8 g Carbohydrates 2.4 g

Sugar 0.5 g Protein 6.6 g Cholesterol 87 mg

Cheesy Garlic Bread Chaffle

Time: 15 minutes Serve: 2

Ingredients:

- 1 egg, lightly beaten

- 1 tsp parsley, minced

- 2 tbsp parmesan cheese, grated

- 1 tbsp butter, melted

- 1/4 tsp garlic powder

- 1/4 tsp baking powder, gluten-free

- 1 tsp coconut flour

- 1/2 cup cheddar cheese, shredded

Directions:

1. Preheat your waffle maker.

2. In a bowl, whisk egg, garlic powder, baking powder, coconut flour, and cheddar cheese until well combined.

3. Spray waffle maker with cooking spray.

4. Pour half of the batter in the hot waffle maker and cook for 3 minutes or until set. Repeat with the remaining batter.

5. Brush chaffles with melted butter.

6. Place chaffles on baking tray and top with parmesan cheese and broil until cheese melted.

7. Garnish with parsley and serve.

Nutrition: Calories 248 Fat 19.4 g Carbohydrates 5.4 g Sugar 1 g

Keto Oreo Chaffles

Preparation Time: 13 minutes Cooking Time: 28 minutes Servings: 4

Ingredients:

For the Oreo chaffles:

- 2 eggs, beaten

- 1 cup finely grated mozzarella cheese

- 2 tbsp almond flour

- 1 tbsp unsweetened dark cocoa powder

- 2 tbsp erythritol

- 1 tbsp cream cheese, softened

- ½ tsp vanilla extract

For the glaze:

- 1 tbsp swerve confectioner's sugar

- 1 tsp water

Directions:

1. Preheat the waffle iron.

2. In a medium bowl, combine all the ingredients for the Oreo chaffles until adequately mixed.

3. Open the iron and pour in a quarter of the batter. Close the iron and cook until crispy, 7 minutes.

4. Remove the chaffle onto a plate and set aside.

5. Make 3 more chaffles with the remaining batter and transfer to a plate to cool.

For the glaze:

1. In a small bowl, whisk the swerve confectioner's sugar and water until smooth.

2. Drizzle a little of the glaze over each chaffle and serve after.

Nutrition: Calories 50; Fats 3.64g; Carbs 1.27g; Net Carbs 0.77g; Protein 3.4g

Fried Pickle Chaffle Sticks

Preparation Time: 10 minutes Cooking Time: 28 minutes Servings: 4

Ingredients:

- 1 egg, beaten

- ¼ cup pork rinds

- ½ cup finely grated mozzarella cheese

- ½ tbsp pickle juice

- 8 thin pickle slices, patted with a paper towel

Directions:

1. Preheat the waffle iron.

2. In a medium bowl, combine the egg, pork rinds, mozzarella cheese, and pickle juice.

3. Open the iron and pour in 2 tbsp of the mixture, lay two pickle slices on top, and cover with 2 tbsp of the batter.

4. Close the iron and cook until brown and crispy, 7 minutes.

5. Remove the chaffle onto a plate and set aside.

6. Make 3 more chaffles in the same manner, using the remaining ingredients.

7. Cut the chaffles into sticks and serve after with cheese dip.

Nutrition: Calories 68; Fats 4.17g; Carbs 2.2g; Net Carbs 2.0g; Protein 5.25g

Keto Chaffle Churro Sticks

Preparation Time: 10 minutes Cooking
Time: 28 minutes Servings: 4

Ingredients:

- 1 egg, beaten

- ½ cup finely grated mozzarella
  cheese

- 2 tbsp swerve brown sugar

- ½ tsp cinnamon powder

Directions:

1. Preheat the waffle iron.

2. Combine all the ingredients in a medium
   bowl until smooth.

3. Open the iron and pour in a quarter of the
   mixture. Close the iron and cook until
   golden brown and crispy, 7 minutes.

4. Remove the chaffle onto a plate and
   set aside.

5. Make 3 more chaffles with the remaining
   ingredients

6. Cut the chaffles into 4 sticks and serve after.

Nutrition: Calories 45; Fats 3.2g; Carbs 1.08g; Net Carbs 0.78g; Protein 2.95g

Cheeseburger Chaffle

Preparation Time: 15 minutes Cooking
Time: 15 minutes Servings: 2

Ingredients:

- 1 lb. ground beef

- 1 onion, minced

- 1 tsp. parsley, chopped

- 1 egg, beaten

- Salt and pepper to taste

- 1 tablespoon olive oil

- 4 basic chaffles

- 2 lettuce leaves

- 2 cheese slices

- 1 tablespoon dill pickles

- Ketchup

- Mayonnaise

Directions:

1. In a large bowl, combine the ground beef, onion, parsley, egg, salt and pepper.

2. Mix well.

3. Form 2 thick patties.

4. Add olive oil to the pan.

5. Place the pan over medium heat.

6. Cook the patty for 3 to 5 minutes per side or until fully cooked.

7. Place the patty on top of each chaffle.

8. Top with lettuce, cheese and pickles.

9. Squirt ketchup and mayo over the patty and veggies.

10. 1Top with another chaffle.

Nutrition:

Calories 325 Total Fat 16.3g Saturated Fat 6.5g Cholesterol 157mg Sodium 208mg Total Carbohydrate 3g Dietary Fiber 0.7g Total Sugars 1.4g Protein 39.6g Potassium 532mg

Sausage Ball Chaffles

Preparation Time: 15 minutes Cooking Time:
28 minutes Servings: 4

Ingredients:

- 1 lb Italian sausage, crumbled

- 3 tbsp almond flour

- 2 tsp baking powder

- 1 egg, beaten

- ¼ cup finely grated Parmesan cheese

- 1 cup finely grated cheddar cheese

Directions:

1. Preheat the waffle iron.

2. Pour all the ingredients into a medium mixing
   bowl and mix well with your hands.

3. Open the iron, lightly grease with cooking
   spray and add 3 tbsp of the sausage mixture.
   Close the iron and cook for 4 minutes.

4. Open the iron, flip the chaffles and cook
   further for 3 minutes.

5. Remove the chaffle onto a plate and

make 3 more using the rest of the
mixture.

6. Cut each chaffle into sticks or quarters
   and enjoy after.

Nutrition: Calories 465; Fats 33.5g; Carbs
10.87g; Net Carbs 7.57g; Protein 32.52g

Garlic Bread Chaffles

Preparation Time: 10 minutes Cooking Time: 14 minutes Servings: 2

Ingredients:

- 1 egg, beaten

- ½ cup finely grated mozzarella cheese
- 1 tsp Italian seasoning

- ½ tsp garlic powder

- 1 tsp chive-flavored cream cheese

Directions:

1. Preheat the waffle iron.

2. Mix all the ingredients in a medium bowl until well combined.

3. Open the iron and add half of the mixture. Close and cook until golden brown and crispy, 7 minutes.

4. Remove the chaffle onto a plate and make a second one with the remaining batter.

5. Cut each chaffle into sticks or quarters and enjoy

after.

Nutrition: Calories 51; Fats 3.56g; Carbs 1.57g; Net Carbs 1.27g; Protein 3.13g

Pumpkin-Cinnamon Churro Sticks

Preparation Time: 10 minutes Cooking Time: 14 minutes Servings: 2

Ingredients:

- 3 tbsp coconut flour

- ¼ cup pumpkin puree

- 1 egg, beaten

- ½ cup finely grated mozzarella cheese

- 2 tbsp sugar-free maple syrup + more for serving

- 1 tsp baking powder

- 1 tsp vanilla extract

- ½ tsp pumpkin spice seasoning
  - 1/8 tsp salt

  - 1 tbsp cinnamon powder

Directions:

1. Preheat the waffle iron.

2. Mix all the ingredients in a medium bowl until well combined.

3. Open the iron and add half of the mixture. Close and cook until golden brown and crispy, 7 minutes.

4. Remove the chaffle onto a plate and make 1 more with the remaining batter.

5. Cut each chaffle into sticks, drizzle the top with more maple syrup and serve after.

Nutrition: Calories 219; Fats 9.72g; Carbs 8.64g; Net Carbs 4.34g; Protein 25.27g

Crunchy Zucchini Chaffle

Time: 20 minutes Serve: 8

Ingredients:

- 2 eggs, lightly beaten
- 1 garlic clove, minced
- 1 1/2 tbsp onion, minced
- 1 cup cheddar cheese, grated
- 1 small zucchini, grated and squeeze out all liquid

Directions:

1. Preheat your waffle maker.

2. In a bowl, mix eggs, garlic, onion, zucchini, and cheese until well combined.

3. Spray waffle maker with cooking spray.

4. Pour 1/4 cup batter in the hot waffle maker and cook for 5 minutes or until golden brown. Repeat with the remaining batter.

5. Serve and enjoy.

Nutrition: Calories 76 Fat 5.8 g
Carbohydrates 1.1 g Sugar 0.5 g
Protein 5.1 g Cholesterol 56 mg

~
7
3
~

Guacamole Chaffle Bites

Preparation Time: 10 minutes Cooking Time: 14 minutes Servings: 2

Ingredients:

- 1 large turnip, cooked and mashed

- 2 bacon slices, cooked and finely chopped

- ½ cup finely grated Monterey Jack cheese

- 1 egg, beaten

- 1 cup guacamole for topping

Directions:

1. Preheat the waffle iron.
2. Mix all the ingredients except for the guacamole in a medium bowl.

3. Open the iron and add half of the mixture. Close and cook for 4 minutes. Open the lid, flip the chaffle and cook further until golden brown and crispy, 3 minutes.

4. Remove the chaffle onto a plate and make another in the same manner.

5. Cut each chaffle into wedges, top with the guacamole and serve afterward.

Nutrition: Calories 311; Fats 22.52g; Carbs 8.29g; Net Carbs 5.79g; Protein 13.62g

Zucchini Parmesan Chaffles

Preparation Time: 10 minutes Cooking
Time: 14 minutes

Servings: 2

Ingredients:

- 1 cup shredded zucchini

- 1 egg, beaten

- ½ cup finely grated Parmesan cheese

- Salt and freshly ground black pepper to taste

Directions:

1. Preheat the waffle iron.

2. Put all the ingredients in a medium bowl
   and mix well.

3. Open the iron and add half of the mixture.
   Close and cook until crispy, 7 minutes.

4. Remove the chaffle onto a plate and make
   another with the remaining mixture.

5. Cut each chaffle into wedges and serve
   afterward.

Nutrition: Calories 138; Fats 9.07g; Carbs 3.81g; Net Carbs 3.71g; Protein 10.02g

Yogurt Chaffles

Serving: 6 chaffles.

Preparation Time: 30 minutes Cooking Time: 0 minutes

Ingredients

- 1-1/4 cups all-purpose flour

- 1-1/2 teaspoons baking powder

- 1 teaspoon baking soda

- 1/4 teaspoon salt

- 2 cups (16 ounces) plain yogurt

- 1/4 cup butter, melted

- 2 eggs

- 2 tablespoons honey

- 1/2 cup mozzarella cheese, shredded
- Raspberry, peach or strawberry yogurt

- Raspberries, blueberries and/or sliced peaches

Direction

In a bowl, combine the flour, baking powder, baking soda and salt. Beat in plain yogurt, butter, eggs mozzarella cheese and honey until smooth. Bake in a preheated waffle iron according to manufacturer's directions until golden brown. Top with flavored yogurt and fruit.

Nutrition: Calories: 516 calories Total Fat: 24g Cholesterol: 204mg Sodium: 1089mg Total Carbohydrate: 59g Protein: 15g Fiber: 1g

Chaffle Fruit Snacks

Preparation Time: 10 minutes
Cooking Time: 14 minutes Servings: 2

Ingredients:

- 1 egg, beaten

- ½ cup finely grated cheddar cheese

- ½ cup Greek yogurt for topping

- 8 raspberries and blackberries for topping

Directions:

1. Preheat the waffle iron.

2. Mix the egg and cheddar cheese in a medium bowl.

3. Open the iron and add half of the mixture. Close and cook until crispy, 7 minutes.

4. Remove the chaffle onto a plate and make another with the remaining mixture.

5. Cut each chaffle into wedges and arrange on a plate.

6. Top each waffle with a tablespoon of yogurt and then two berries.

   7. Serve afterward.

Nutrition: Calories 207; Fats 15.29g; Carbs 4.36g; Net Carbs 3.86g; Protein 12.91g

Red Velvet Chaffle Cake

Preparation Time: 15 minutes Cooking
Time: 28 minutes Servings: 4

Ingredients:

For the chaffles:

- 2 eggs, beaten

- ½ cup finely grated Parmesan cheese

- 2 oz cream cheese, softened

- 2 drops red food coloring

- 1 tsp vanilla extract

For the frosting:

- 3 tbsp cream cheese, softened

- 1 tbsp sugar-free maple syrup

- ¼ tsp vanilla extract

Directions:

For the chaffles:

1. Preheat the waffle iron.

2. In a medium bowl, mix all the ingredients for the chaffles.

3. Open the iron and add a quarter of the mixture. Close and cook until crispy, 7 minutes.

4. Transfer the chaffle to a plate and make 3 more chaffles with the remaining batter.

For the frosting:

1. In a medium bowl, using a hand mixer, whisk the cream cheese, maple syrup, and vanilla extract until smooth.

2. Assemble the chaffles with the frosting to make the cake.

3. Slice and serve.

Nutrition: Calories 147; Fats 9.86g; Carbs 5.22g; Net Carbs 5.22g; Protein 8.57g

Almond Butter Chaffle Cake with Chocolate Butter Frosting

Preparation Time: 20 minutes Cooking Time: 28 minutes Servings: 4

Ingredients:

For the chaffles:

- 1 egg, beaten

- ⅓ cup finely grated mozzarella cheese
- 1 tbsp almond flour

- 2 tbsp almond butter

- 1 tbsp swerve confectioner's sugar

- ½ tsp vanilla extract

For the chocolate butter frosting:

- 1½ cups butter, room temperature

- 1 cup unsweetened cocoa powder

- ½ cup almond milk

- 5 cups swerve confectioner's sugar

- 2 tsp vanilla extract

Directions:

For the chaffles:

1. Preheat the waffle iron.

2. In a medium bowl, mix the egg, mozzarella cheese, almond flour, almond butter, swerve confectioner's sugar, and vanilla extract.

3. Open the iron and add a quarter of the mixture. Close

   and cook until crispy, 7 minutes.

4. Transfer the chaffle to a plate and make 3 more chaffles with the remaining batter.

For the frosting:

1. In a medium bowl, cream the butter and cocoa powder until smooth.

2. Gradually, whisk in the almond milk and swerve confectioner's sugar until smooth.

3. Add the vanilla extract and mix well.

4. Assemble the chaffles with the frosting to

make the cake.

5. **Slice and serve.**

Nutrition: Calories 838; Fats 85.35g; Carbs 8.73g; Net Carbs 2.03g; Protein 13.59g

Cinnamon Chaffles with Custard Filling

Preparation Time: 25 minutes Cooking Time: 28 minutes Servings: 4

Ingredients:

For the custard filling:

- 4 egg yolks, beaten

- 1 tbsp erythritol

- ¼ tsp xanthan gum

- 1 cup heavy cream

- 1 tbsp vanilla extract

For the chaffles:

- 2 eggs, beaten

- 2 tbsp cream cheese, softened

- 1 cup finely grated Monterey Jack cheese

- 1 tsp vanilla extract

- 1 tbsp heavy cream

- 1 tbsp coconut flour

- ½ tsp baking powder

- ½ tsp ground cinnamon

- ¼ tsp erythritol

Directions:

For the custard filling:

1. In a medium bowl, beat the egg yolks with the erythritol. Mix in the xanthan gum until smooth.

2. Pour the heavy cream into a medium saucepan and simmer over low heat. Pour the mixture into the egg mixture while whisking vigorously until well mixed.

3. Transfer the mixture to the saucepan and continue whisking while cooking over low heat until thickened, 20 to 30 seconds. Turn the heat off and stir in the vanilla extract.

4. Strain the custard through a

fine-mesh into a bowl. Cover the bowl
with plastic wrap.

5. Refrigerate for 1 hour.

For the chaffles:

1. After 1 hour, preheat the waffle iron.

2. In a medium bowl, mix all the ingredients
   for the chaffles.

3. Open the iron and add a quarter of the
   mixture. Close and cook until crispy, 7
   minutes.

4. Transfer the chaffle to a plate and make
   3 more with the remaining batter.

To serve:

Spread the custard filling between two chaffle
quarters, sandwich and enjoy!

Nutrition: Calories 239; Fats 21.25g; Carbs 3.21g;
Net Carbs 3.01g; Protein 6.73g

Tiramisu Chaffles

Preparation Time: 20 minutes Cooking
Time: 28 minutes Servings: 4

Ingredients:

For the chaffles:

- 2 eggs, beaten

- 3 tbsp cream cheese, softened

- ½ cup finely grated Gouda cheese

- 1 tsp vanilla extract

- 1/4 tsp erythritol

For the coffee syrup:

- 2 tbsp strong coffee, room temperature

- 3 tbsp sugar-free maple syrup

For the filling:

- ¼ cup heavy cream
- 2 tsp vanilla extract

- ¼ tsp erythritol

- 4 tbsp mascarpone cheese, room

temperature

- 1 tbsp cream cheese, softened

For dusting:

- ½ tsp unsweetened cocoa powder

Directions:

For the chaffles:

1. Preheat the waffle iron.

2. In a medium bowl, mix all the ingredients for the chaffles.

3. Open the iron and add a quarter of the mixture. Close and cook until crispy, 7 minutes.

4. Transfer the chaffle to a plate and make 3 more with the remaining batter.

For the coffee syrup:

In a small bowl, mix the coffee and maple syrup. Set aside.

For the filling:

1. Beat the heavy cream, vanilla, and erythritol in a medium bowl using an electric hand mixer until stiff peak forms.

2. In another bowl, beat the mascarpone cheese and cream cheese until well combined. Add the heavy cream mixture and fold in. Spoon the mixture into a piping bag.

To assemble:

1. Spoon 1 tbsp of the coffee syrup on one chaffle and pipe some of the cream cheese mixture on top. Cover with another chaffle and continue the assembling process.

2. Generously dust with cocoa powder and refrigerate overnight.

3. When ready to enjoy, slice and serve.

Nutrition: Calories 208; Fats 15.91g; Carbs 4.49g; Net Carbs 4.39g; Protein 10.1g

Okonomiyaki Chaffles

Preparation Time: 20 minutes Cooking
Time: 28 minutes Servings: 4

Ingredients:

For the chaffles:

- 2 eggs, beaten

- 1 cup finely grated mozzarella cheese

- ½ tsp baking powder

- ¼ cup shredded radishes

For the sauce:

- 2 tsp coconut aminos

- 2 tbsp sugar-free ketchup

- 1 tbsp sugar-free maple syrup
  - 2 tsp Worcestershire sauce

For the topping:

- 1 tbsp mayonnaise

- 2 tbsp chopped fresh scallions

- 2 tbsp bonito flakes

- 1 tsp dried seaweed powder

- 1 tbsp pickled ginger

Directions:

For the chaffles:

1. Preheat the waffle iron.

2. In a medium bowl, mix the eggs, mozzarella cheese, baking powder, and radishes.

3. Open the iron and add a quarter of the mixture. Close and cook until crispy, 7 minutes.

4. Transfer the chaffle to a plate and make a 3 more chaffles in the same manner.

For the sauce:

Combine the coconut aminos, ketchup, maple syrup, and Worcestershire sauce in a medium bowl and mix well.

For the topping:

In another mixing bowl, mix the mayonnaise, scallions, bonito flakes, seaweed powder, and ginger

To serve:

Arrange the chaffles on four different plates and swirl the sauce on top. Spread the topping on the chaffles and serve afterward.

Nutrition: Calories 90; Fats 3.32g; Carbs 2.97g; Net Carbs 2.17g; Protein 12.09g

Perfect Jalapeno Chaffle

Time: 20 minutes Serve: 6

Ingredients:

- 3 eggs

- 1 cup cheddar cheese, shredded
- 8 oz cream cheese

- 2 jalapeno peppers, diced

- 4 bacon slices, cooked and crumbled

- 1/2 tsp baking powder

- 3 tbsp coconut flour

- 1/4 tsp sea salt

Directions:

1. Preheat your waffle maker.

2. In a small bowl, mix coconut flour, baking powder, and salt.

3. In a medium bowl, beat cream cheese using a hand mixer until fluffy.

4. In a large bowl, beat eggs until fluffy.

5. Add cheddar cheese and half cup cream in eggs and beat until well combined.

6. Add coconut flour mixture to egg mixture and mix until combined.

7. Add jalapeno pepper and stir well.

8. Spray waffle maker with cooking spray.

9. Pour 1/4 cup batter in the hot waffle maker and cook for 4-5 minutes. Repeat with the remaining batter.

10. Once chaffle is slightly cool then top with remaining cream cheese and bacon.

11. Serve and enjoy.

Nutrition: **Calories 340 Fat 28 g**
Carbohydrates 6.2 g Sugar 1 g
Protein 16.1 g Cholesterol 157 mg

French Onion Soup Chaffles

Preparation Time: 10 minutes Cooking
Time: 28 minutes Servings: 4

Ingredients:

- 2 eggs, beaten

- 1 cup finely grated Gruyere cheese

- 1/3 cup cream cheese, softened

- ¼ cup caramelized onions

- Salt and freshly ground black pepper to taste

- 1/6 tsp dried thyme

- 2 tbsp chopped fresh chives to garnish

Directions:

1. Preheat the waffle iron.

2. In a medium bowl, mix all the ingredients except the chives.

3. Open the iron and add a quarter of the mixture. Close and cook until crispy, 7 minutes.

4. Transfer the chaffle to a plate and make 3 more chaffles in the same manner.

5. Garnish the chaffles with the chives and serve afterward.

Nutrition: Calories 230; Fats 18.45g; Carbs 1.71g; Net Carbs 1.51g; Protein 14.14g

Chaffle with Sausage Gravy

Preparation Time: 5 minutes Cooking
Time: 15 minutes Servings: 2

Ingredients:

- ¼ cup sausage, cooked

- 3 tablespoons chicken broth

- 2 teaspoons cream cheese

- 2 tablespoons heavy whipping cream

- ¼ teaspoon garlic powder

- Pepper to taste

- 2 basic chaffles

Directions:

1. Add the sausage, broth, cream cheese, cream, garlic powder and pepper to a pan over medium heat.

2. Bring to a boil and then reduce heat.

3. Simmer for 10 minutes or until the sauce has thickened.

4. Pour the gravy on top of the basic chaffles

5. Serve.

Nutrition:

Calories 212 Total Fat 17 g Saturated Fat 10 g
Cholesterol 134 mg Sodium 350 mg Potassium 133 mg
Total Carbohydrate 3 g Dietary Fiber 1 g Protein 11 g
Total Sugars 1 g

Broccoli & Cheese Chaffle

Preparation Time: 5 minutes Cooking
Time: 8 minutes Servings: 2

Ingredients:

- ¼ cup broccoli florets

- 1 egg, beaten

- 1 tablespoon almond flour

- ¼ teaspoon garlic powder

- ½ cup cheddar cheese

Directions:

1. Preheat your waffle maker.

2. Add the broccoli to the food processor.

3. Pulse until chopped.

4. Add to a bowl.

5. Stir in the egg and the rest of the ingredients.

6. Mix well.

7. Pour half of the batter to the waffle maker.

8. Cover and cook for 4 minutes.

9. Repeat procedure to make the next chaffle.

   Nutrition: Calories 170 Total Fat 13 g Saturated Fat 7 g Cholesterol 112 mg Sodium 211 mg Potassium 94 mg Total Carbohydrate 2 g Dietary Fiber 1 g Protein 11 g Total Sugars 1 g

Pumpkin & Pecan Chaffle

Preparation Time: 5 minutes Cooking
Time: 10 minutes Servings: 2

Ingredients:

- 1 egg, beaten

- ½ cup mozzarella cheese, grated

- ½ teaspoon pumpkin spice

- 1 tablespoon pureed pumpkin

- 2 tablespoons almond flour

- 1 teaspoon sweetener

- 2 tablespoons pecans, chopped

Directions:

1. Turn on the waffle maker.
2. Beat the egg in a bowl.

3. Stir in the rest of the
   ingredients.

4. Pour half of the mixture into the device.

5. Seal the lid.

6. Cook for 5 minutes.

7. Remove the chaffle carefully.

8. Repeat the steps to make the second chaffle.

Nutrition: Calories 210 Total Fat 17 g Saturated Fat 10 g Cholesterol 110
mg Sodium 250 mg Potassium 570 mg Total Carbohydrate 4.6 g Dietary Fiber 1.7 g Protein 11 g Total Sugars 2 g

Spicy Shrimp and Chaffles

Preparation Time: 15 minutes
Cooking Time: 31 minutes Servings: 4

Ingredients:

For the shrimp:

- 1 tbsp olive oil

- 1 lb jumbo shrimp, peeled and deveined

- 1 tbsp Creole seasoning

- Salt to taste

- 2 tbsp hot sauce

- 3 tbsp butter

- 2 tbsp chopped fresh scallions to garnish

For the chaffles:

- 2 eggs, beaten

- 1 cup finely grated Monterey Jack cheese

Directions:

For the shrimp:

1. Heat the olive oil in a medium skillet over medium heat.

2. Season the shrimp with the Creole seasoning and salt. Cook in the oil until pink and opaque on both sides, 2

   minutes.

3. Pour in the hot sauce and butter. Mix well until the shrimp is adequately coated in the sauce, 1 minute.

4. Turn the heat off and set aside.

For the chaffles:

1. Preheat the waffle iron.

2. In a medium bowl, mix the eggs and Monterey Jack cheese.

3. Open the iron and add a quarter of the mixture. Close and cook until crispy, 7 minutes.

4. Transfer the chaffle to a plate and make 3 more chaffles in the same manner.

5. Cut the chaffles into quarters and place on a plate.

6. Top with the shrimp and garnish with the scallions.

7. Serve warm.

Nutrition: Calories 342 Fats 19.75g Carbs 2.8g Net Carbs 2.3g Protein 36.01g

Apple Pie Chaffles

Preparation Time: 10 minutes Cooking
Time: 14 minutes Servings: 2

Ingredients:

- ½ cup finely grated mozzarella
  cheese

- 1 egg, beaten

- ¼ tsp apple pie spice

- 4 butter slices for serving

Directions:

1. Preheat the waffle iron.

2. Open the iron, pour in half of the
   mozzarella cheese in the iron, top with half
   of the egg, and sprinkle with half of the
   apple pie spice.

3. Close the iron and cook until crispy, 6 to 7
   minutes.

4. Remove the chaffle onto a plate and set
   aside.

5. Make the second chaffle with the

remaining ingredients.

6. Allow cooling and serve after.

Nutrition: Calories 146; Fats 14.73g; Carbs 0.9g; Net Carbs 0.7g; Protein 3.07g

Keto Reuben Chaffles

Preparation Time: 15 minutes Cooking
Time: 28 minutes Servings: 4

Ingredients:

For the chaffles:

- 2 eggs, beaten
- 1 cup finely grated Swiss cheese
- 2 tsp caraway seeds
- 1/8 tsp salt
- ½ tsp baking powder

For the sauce:

- 2 tbsp sugar-free ketchup
- 3 tbsp mayonnaise
- 1 tbsp dill relish
- 1 tsp hot sauce

For the filling:

- 6 oz pastrami
- 2 Swiss cheese slices
- ¼ cup pickled radishes

Directions:

For the chaffles:

1. Preheat the waffle iron.

2. In a medium bowl, mix the eggs, Swiss cheese, caraway seeds, salt, and baking powder.

3. Open the iron and add a quarter of the mixture. Close and cook until crispy, 7 minutes.

4. Transfer the chaffle to a plate and make 3 more chaffles in the same manner.

For the sauce:

1. In another bowl, mix the ketchup, mayonnaise, dill relish, and hot sauce.

2. To assemble:

3. Divide on two chaffles; the sauce, the pastrami, Swiss cheese slices, and pickled radishes.

4. Cover with the other chaffles, divide the sandwich in halves and serve.

Nutrition: Calories 316 Fats 21.78g Carbs 6.52g Net Carbs 5.42g Protein 23.56g

Herb Bread

<u>Serves: 4</u>

<u>Ingredients:</u>

- 2 Tbsp Coconut Flour

- 1 ½ cups Almond Flour

- 2 Tbsp Fresh Herbs of choice, chopped

- 2 Tbsp Ground Flax Seeds

- 1 ½ tsp Baking Soda

- ¼ tsp Salt

- 5 Eggs

- 1 Tbsp Apple Cider Vinegar

- ¼ cup Coconut Oil, melted

<u>Directions:</u>

1. Preheat your oven to 350F / 175C. Grease a loaf pan and set aside.

2. Add the coconut flour, almond flour, herbs, flax, baking soda, and salt to your food processor. Pulse to combine and then add the eggs, vinegar, and oil.

3. Transfer the batter to the prepared loaf pan and bake in the preheated oven for about 30 min.

4. Once baked and golden brown, remove from the oven, set aside to cool, slice and eat.

<u>Nutritional Values:</u>

Calories: 421,

Total Fat: 37.4 g, Saturated Fat: 14.8 g, Carbs:

9.4 g, Sugars: 0.9 g, Protein: 15.1 g

Almond Keto Bread

Ingredients:

- 3 cups Almond Flour

- 1 tsp Baking Soda

- 2 tsp Baking Powder

- ¼ tsp Salt
¼ cup Almond Milk

- ½ cup + 2 Tbsp Olive Oil

- 3 Eggs

Serves: 10 slices Nutritional

Values: Calories: 302,

Total Fat: 28.6 g, Saturated Fat: 3

g, Carbs: 7.3g,

Sugars: 1.2 g,

Protein: 8.5 g

Directions:

1. Preheat your oven to 300F / 149C. Grease a loaf pan (e.g. 9x5) and set aside.
2. Combine all the ingredients and transfer the batter to the prepared loaf pan.
3. Bake in the preheated oven for an hour.
4. Once baked, remove from the oven, allow to cool, slice and eat.

Almond Bread

Nutritional Values:

Calories: 277,

Total Fat: 21.5 g, Saturated Fat:

7.3 g, Carbs: 12.7 g,

Sugars: 0.3 g, Protein: 10.7 g

Ingredients:

- 1 1/4 cups Almond Flour

- 1/2 cup Coconut Flour

- 1/4 cup Ground Chia Seeds

- 1/2 tsp Baking Soda

- 1/4 tsp Salt

- 4 Tbsp Coconut Oil, melted

- 5 Eggs

- 1 Tbsp Apple Cider Vinegar

Directions:

1. Preheat your oven to 350F / 190C. Grease a loaf pan and set aside.
2. Combine all the dry ingredients and set aside.
3. Mix together the wet ingredients and add them to the dry ingredients. Mix well to combine.
4. Transfer the batter to the prepared loaf pan and bake in the preheated oven for about 40-50 minutes.
5. When   baked,   allow   to   cool, slice   and   eat.

Thanksgiving Bread

Ingredients:

- 1 Tbsp Ghee

- 2 Celery Stalks, chopped

- 1 Onion, chopped

- ½ cup Walnuts

- ½ cup Coconut Flour

- 1½ cup Almond Flour

- 1 Tbsp Fresh Rosemary, chopped

- 10 Sage Leaves, finely chopped

- 1 tsp Baking Soda

- 1 pinch Freshly Grated Nutmeg
- ¼ tsp Salt½ cup Chicken Broth

- 4 Eggs

- 2-3 Bacon Strips, cooked and crumbled

Serves: 4

Nutritional Values:

Calories: 339, Total Fat: 26.9 g, Protein: 12.2 g`
Saturated Fat: 5.7 g, Carbs: 16.7 g,

Sugars: 1.2 g,

Directions:

1. Preheat your oven to 350F / 175C.

2. Add the ghee to a pan and melt on medium. Add the celery and onion and sauté for about 5 minutes.

3. Once tender, add the walnuts and cook for a few more minutes. Set aside.

4. In a bowl, mix together the coconut flour, almond flour, rosemary, sage, baking soda, nutmeg, and salt.

5. Mix in the sautéed celery and onion and add the chicken broth and eggs. Mix until well incorporated.

6. Stir in the bacon crumbles and transfer the batter to the prepared loaf pan. Bake n the preheated oven for about 30-35 minutes.

7. Once baked, leave to cool, slice and serve.

Keto Rosemary Rolls

Ingredients:

1 cup almond flour

1 tbsp baking powder 2

tsp fresh rosemary 1 tsp

dried chives

4 oz cream cheese

3/4 cup mozzarella cheese, shredded

1 egg

Cooking time: 20 min Serves : 8 rolls

Nutritional Values: Calories per roll: 89 Carbs

2.3g,

Total Fat: 7.7g, Protein: 3.3g

Directions:

1. Heat oven to 160°C.

2. Mix all dry ingredients: almond flour+baking powder+dried chives+fresh rosemary.

3. Microwave mozzarella+cream cheese for a minute.

4. Add there an egg and mix again.

5. Add to the egg with cheese mixed dry ingredients and make the dough.

6. Let it cool in a freezer for 15 min.

7. Oil your hands and form 8 small balls

8. Put them on a baking tray covered with the butter paper.

9. Bake for 20 min.

Soft Dinner Rolls

Cooking time: 20 min Servings: 12 (2 rolls per serving)

Nutritional Values:

Calories per serving: 157 Carbs: 4.5g,

Total Fat: 13.2g, Proteins: 6.6g.

Ingredients:

- 10 oz almond flour
- ¼ cup baking powder
- 1 cup cream cheese
- 3 cups mozzarella, shredded
- 4 eggs
- 1 tbsp butter

Steps:

1. Heat the oven to 190°C

2. Microwave mozzarella+cream cheese for a minute.

3. Mix all dry ingredients: almond flour+baking powder+eggs

4. Add cheeses to dry ingredients, mix well and put aside for 15 min.

5. Form 12 rolls and let them cool in the freezer for 7-10 min.

6. Melt the butter in the iron skillet.

7. Put the rolls next to each other and bake for 20 min in the skillet.

8. Enjoy

Notes:

☐ **So much quantity of baking powder will help the dough to rise well and not be flat.**

Hot Dog Rolls

Ingredients:

- 6 oz almond flour

- ½ tbsp. baking powder

- 3 eggs

- 4 tbsp oil

- salt

Cooking time: 3 min Yield: 3 buns

Nutrition facts: Calories per bun: 274

Carbs 2.6g,

Fats 28.3g, Proteins: 7.8g.

Steps:

1. Combine all the ingredients together: almond flour+ baking powder+eggs+oil+salt.Mix them well.

2. Microwave this mixture fo 1,5-2 min. Check it. If it is wet somewhere, microwave it for more 30 sec.

3. Cut from the bread the roll for your hot dogs.

4. Create the stuffing you like and enjoy.

Keto Hot Dog Buns

<u>Ingredients:</u>

- 10 oz almond flour

- 1/3 cup psyllium husk powder

- 2 tsp baking powder

- 1 tsp sea salt

- 2 tsp cider vinegar

- 10 oz boiling water

- 3 egg whites

<u>Cooking time: 45 min</u> <u>Yield: 10 rolls</u>

<u>Nutrition facts:</u> Calories per bun: 29

Carbs 1.5g,

Fats 2.1g, Proteins: 1.3g.

Steps:

1. Heat the oven to 175°C.

2. Mix all dry ingredients: almond flour+ psyllium husk powder+ baking powder+ sea salt.

3. Boil the water.

4. Add to dry ingredients: water+ vinegar+ egg whites and whisk. The dough should be soft.

   5. Form 10 hot dog buns.

   6. Put them on the baking tray covered with the butter paper.

   7. Bake for 45 min.

   8. Create the stuffing you like and enjoy.

Cheese Muffins

Cooking time: 25 min Yield: 8

muffins Nutrition facts: Calories

per muffin: 122 Carbs 1.9g,

Fats 9.1g, Proteins:

9.7 g.

Ingredients:

- 4 oz almond flour

- ½ tsp baking soda

- ½ tsp sea salt

- ½ tsp garlic powder

- ¼ tsp cayenne

- 3 eggs

- 6 oz cheddar cheese, shredded

- 1.5 oz parmesan, grated

Steps:

1. Heat the oven to 160 C.

2. Whisk together: eggs+salt+garlic powder+cayenne.

3. Add there: almond flour+ baking soda+ cheeses. Mix well. The dough should be soft.

4. Prepare your silicone cups, grease them. Or use paper cups.

5. Put the dough into each cup approx. 4 tbsp per cup.

6. Bake for 25 min.

7. Cool before serving.

One Minute Muffin

Ingredients:

- 2 tbsp flaxseed meal

- 2 tbsp almond flour

- ½ tsp baking powder

- Salt

- 1 egg

- 1 tsp oil

Cooking time: 1 min

Yield: 1 cup Nutrition

facts: Calories per cup:

377 Carbs 6.3g,

Fats 15g, Proteins: 8.9g.

<u>Steps:</u>

1. Mix together dry ingredients: flaxseed meal+almond flour+baking powder+salt.

2. Add there an egg+oil. Mix well.

3. Microwave for 1 min. Or bake at 175 C for 15 min.

4. E

n

j

o

y

.

N

o

t

e

:

⌐ **The ratio is half flax and half almond flour. Instead of flax you can use almond flour 100% or flaxseed meal 100% or coconut flour 100%**

Keto Flaxseed Cinnamon Bun Muffins

Ingredients:

- 2 cups flaxseed meal

- 25 drops stevia

- 1 tbsp baking powder

- 2 tbsp cinnamon,ground

- ½ tbsp salt

- 5 eggs

- ½ cup water, room temperature

- 8 tbsp coconut oil, melted

- 2 tsp vanilla extract

Cooking time: 15 min Yield: 12 muffins

Nutrition facts: Calories per muffin: 209 Carbs 7.1g,

Fats 16.8g, Proteins: 5.8g.

Steps:

1. Heat the oven to 170 C.

2. Mix together dry ingredients: flaxseed meal+sweetener+baking powder+ cinnamon+salt.

3. Put together: eggs+ water+oil+vanilla extract. Blend for 30 sec. The mixture should be foamy.

4. Add dry mixture to the foamy and stir well.

5. Meanwhile prepare your silicone cups, grease them.

6. Put the dough into the cups. Approx. 4 tbsp per cup.

7. Bake for 15 min.

Keto Strawberry Muffins

Cooking time: 20 min Yield: 12 muffins Nutrition

facts: Calories: 87

Carbs 4.3g, Fats 7g, Proteins: 2.4g.

Ingredients:

- 10,5 oz almond flour

- 2 tsp baking powder

- 1/4 tsp salt

- 1 tsp cinnamon

- 8 tbsp sweetener

- 5 tbsp butter, melted

- 3 eggs

- 1 tsp vanilla extract

- 6 tbsp heavy cream

- 2/3 cup fresh strawberries

Steps:

1. Heat the oven to 175 C.

2. Beat together: melted butter+sweetener.

3. Add there: eggs+vanilla+cream. Go on beating until the dough is foamy.

4. Mix some sweetener with strawberries and put aside.

5. Sift together: almond flour+baking powder+salt+cinnamon.

6. Add the dry ingredients to the butter and eggs. Mix well.

7. Mix in strawberries.

8. Place the dough into the baking cups, greased.

9. Bake for 20 min.

Keto Cheeseburger Muffin

Cooking time: 23 min Yield: 9 muffins Nutrition facts: Calories per muffin: 96 Carbs 3.7g,

Fats 7g, Proteins: 3.9g.

Ingredients:

- 8 tbsp almond flour
- 8 tbsp flaxseed meal
- 1 tsp baking powder
- ½ tspsalt
- ¼ tsp pepper
- 2 eggs
- 4 tbsp sour cream

Hamburger Filling:

- 1 lb ground beef
- 2 tbsp tomato paste
- Salt, pepper,onion powder,garlic powder to taste

Toppings:

- 1.5 oz cheddar cheese

- 1 pickle, sliced

- 2 tbsp ketchup

- 2 tbsp mustard

Steps:

1. Heat the oven to 175 C.

2. Combine together: ground beef+seasoning+salt+pepper. Fry

3. Mix together the dry ingredients: almond flour+flaxseed meal+baking powder+salt+pepper.

4. Put there:sour cream+eggs

5. Place the dough into the baking silicone cups, greased. Leave some space at the top.

6. Put the ground beef on the top of the dough.

7. Bake for 20 min.

8. Take out of the oven and place the cheese on the ground beef. Bake for 3 min more.

9. Put the topping and enjoy.

Cloud Bread

Cooking time: 30 min **Yield: 8 clouds**

Nutrition facts: Calories per cloud: 37 Carbs 0.3g,

Fats 3g, Proteins: 2.4g.

Ingredients:

- 1/4 tsp cream of tartar

- 3 eggs

- 3 tbsp cream cheese

Steps:

1. Heat the oven to 170 C.

2. Prepare the baking sheet.

3. Separate the egg whites from yolks and beat with tartar cream for 2-3 min using a hand mixer until stiff peaks.

4. Mix yolks and cream cheese separately.

5. Combine whites with yolks softly.

6. Form 8 mounds and place the dough onto the baking sheet, greased.

7. Bake for 30 min.

Spicy Cloud Bread

- 3 eggs

- 4 tbsp xylitol

- 2 tbsp cream cheese

- 2 tsp cinnamon, ground

- ½ tsp baking powder

- vanilla to taste

Cooking time: 25-30 min

Yield: 6 clouds

Nutrition facts:

Calories per bun: 52   Carbs

2.8g, Fats 3.4g,   Proteins:

3.1g.

Steps:

1. Heat the oven to 175 C.

2. Prepare the baking sheet.

3. Separate the egg whites from yolks and beat with baking powder for 2-3 min using a hand mixer until stiff peaks.

4. Mix yolks+cream cheese+vanilla+xylitol+cinnamon.

5. Combine whites with yolks softly.

6. Form 6 mounds and place the dough onto the baking sheet, greased. Make them flat.

7. Bake for 30 min until they are golden.

RECIPES

Chocolate Melt Chaffles

Preparation Time: 15 minutes Cooking Time: 36 minutes Servings: 4

Ingredients

For the chaffles:

- 2 eggs, beaten

- ¼ cup finely grated Gruyere cheese

- 2 tbsp heavy cream

- 1 tbsp coconut flour

- 2 tbsp cream cheese, softened

- 3 tbsp unsweetened cocoa powder

- 2 tsp vanilla extract

- A pinch of salt

    For the chocolate sauce:

- 1/3 cup + 1 tbsp heavy cream

- 1 ½ oz unsweetened baking chocolate,

chopped

- 1 ½ tsp sugar-free maple syrup

- 1 ½ tsp vanilla extract

Directions: *For the chaffles:*

1. Preheat the waffle iron.

2. In a medium bowl, mix all the ingredients for the chaffles.

3. Open the iron and add a quarter of the mixture. Close and cook until crispy, 7 minutes.

4. Transfer the chaffle to a plate and make 3 more with the remaining batter.

5. For the chocolate sauce:

6. **Pour the heavy cream into**saucepan and simmer over low heat, 3 minutes.

7. Turn the heat off and add the chocolate. Allow melting for a few minutes and stir until fully melted, 5 minutes.

8. Mix in the maple syrup and vanilla extract.

9. Assemble the chaffles in layers with the chocolate sauce sandwiched between each layer.

10. Slice and serve immediately.

Nutrition: **Calories 172 Fats 13.57g Carbs 6.65g Net Carbs 3.65g Protein 5.76g**

Chaffles with Keto Ice Cream

Preparation Time: 10 minutes Cooking Time: 14 minutes

Servings: 2

Ingredients:

- 1 egg, beaten

- ½ cup finely grated mozzarella cheese

- ¼ cup almond flour

- 2 tbsp swerve confectioner's sugar

- 1/8 tsp xanthan gum

- Low-carb ice cream (flavor of your choice) for serving

Directions:

1. Preheat the waffle iron.

2. In a medium bowl, mix all the ingredients except the ice cream.

3. Open the iron and add half of the mixture. Close and cook until crispy, 7 minutes.

4. Transfer the chaffle to a plate and make second one with the remaining batter.

5. On each chaffle, add a scoop of low carb ice cream, fold into half-moons and enjoy.

Nutrition: Calories 89 Fats 6.48g Carbs 1.67g Net Carbs 1.37g Protein 5.91g

Strawberry Shortcake Chaffle Bowls

Preparation Time: 10 minutes Cooking Time: 28 minutes Servings: 4

Ingredients:

- 1 egg, beaten

- ½ cup finely grated mozzarella cheese

- 1 tbsp almond flour

- ¼ tsp baking powder

- 2 drops cake batter extract

- 1 cup cream cheese, softened

- 1 cup fresh strawberries, sliced

- 1 tbsp sugar-free maple syrup

Directions:

1. Preheat a waffle bowl maker and grease lightly with cooking spray.

2. Meanwhile, in a medium bowl, whisk all the ingredients except the cream cheese and strawberries.

3. Open the iron, pour in half of the mixture, cover, and cook until crispy, 6 to 7 minutes.

4. Remove the chaffle bowl onto a plate and set aside.

5. Make a second chaffle bowl with the remaining batter.

6. To serve, divide the cream cheese into the chaffle bowls and top with the strawberries.

7. Drizzle the filling with the maple syrup and serve.

Nutrition: Calories 235 Fats 20.62g Carbs 5.9g Net Carbs 5g Protein 7.51g

Chaffles with Raspberry Syrup

Preparation Time: 10 minutes Cooking Time: 38 minutes Servings: 4

Ingredients:

For the chaffles:

- 1 egg, beaten

- ½ cup finely shredded cheddar cheese

- 1 tsp almond flour

- 1 tsp sour cream

For the raspberry syrup:

- 1 cup fresh raspberries

- ¼ cup swerve sugar

- ¼ cup water

- 1 tsp vanilla extract

Directions:

For the chaffles:

1. Preheat the waffle iron.

2. Meanwhile, in a medium bowl, mix the egg, cheddar cheese, almond flour, and sour cream.

3. Open the iron, pour in half of the mixture, cover, and cook until crispy, 7 minutes.

4. Remove the chaffle onto a plate and make another with the remaining batter.

For the raspberry syrup:

1. Meanwhile, add the raspberries, swerve sugar, water, and vanilla extract to a medium pot. Set over low heat and cook until the raspberries soften and sugar becomes syrupy. Occasionally stir while mashing the raspberries as you go. Turn the heat off when your desired consistency is achieved and set aside to cool.

2. Drizzle some syrup on the chaffles and enjoy when ready.

Nutrition: Calories 105 Fats 7.11g Carbs 4.31g Net Carbs 2.21g Protein 5.83g

Blueberry Chaffles

Preparation Time: 10 minutes Cooking Time: 28 minutes Servings: 4

Ingredients:

- 1 egg, beaten

- ½ cup finely grated mozzarella cheese

- 1 tbsp cream cheese, softened

- 1 tbsp sugar-free maple syrup + extra for topping

- ½ cup blueberries

- ¼ tsp vanilla extract

Directions:

1. Preheat the waffle iron.

2. In a medium bowl, mix all the ingredients.

3. Open the iron, lightly grease with cooking spray and pour in a quarter of the mixture.

4. Close the iron and cook until golden brown and crispy, 7 minutes.

5. Remove the chaffle onto a plate and set aside.

6. Make the remaining chaffles with the remaining mixture.

7. Drizzle the chaffles with maple syrup and serve afterward.

Nutrition: Calories 137 Fats 9.07g Carbs 4.02g Net Carbs 3.42g Protein 9.59g

Carrot Chaffle Cake

Preparation Time: 15 minutes Cooking Time: 24 minutes Servings: 6

Ingredients:

- 1 egg, beaten

- 2 tablespoons melted butter

- ½ cup carrot, shredded

- ¾ cup almond flour

- 1 teaspoon baking powder

- 2 tablespoons heavy whipping cream

- 2 tablespoons sweetener

- 1 tablespoon walnuts, chopped

- 1 teaspoon pumpkin spice
- 2 teaspoons cinnamon

Directions:

1. Preheat your waffle maker.

2. In a large bowl, combine all the ingredients.

3. Pour some of the mixture into the waffle maker.

4. Close and cook for 4 minutes.

5. Repeat steps until all the remaining batter has been used.

Nutrition: Calories 294 Total Fat 26.7g Saturated Fat 12g Cholesterol 133mg Sodium 144mg Potassium 421mg Total Carbohydrate 11.6g Dietary Fiber 4.5g Protein 6.8g Total Sugars 1.7g

Wednesday Chaffles

Serving: 24

Preparation Time: 10 minutes Cooking Time: 55 minutes

Ingredients

- cooking spray

- 8 eggs, beaten

- 7 cups water

- 1 cup canola oil

- 1 cup unsweetened applesauce

- 4 teaspoons vanilla extract

- 4 cups whole wheat pastry flour

- 2 cups dry milk powder

- 1/2 cup mozzarella cheese, shredded

- 2 cups flax seed meal

- 1 cup wheat germ

- 1 cup all-purpose flour

- 1/4 cup baking powder

- 4 teaspoons baking powder

- 1/4 cup white sugar

- 1 tablespoon ground cinnamon

- 1 teaspoon salt

Direction

1. Spray a waffle iron with cooking spray and preheat according to manufacturer's instructions.

2. Beat eggs, water, canola oil, applesauce, and vanilla extract in a large bowl thoroughly combined. Add mozzarella cheese and stir well.

3. Whisk whole wheat pastry flour, dry milk powder, flax seed meal, wheat germ, all-purpose flour, 1/4 cup plus 4 teaspoons baking powder, sugar, cinnamon, and salt in a separate large bowl until thoroughly combined. Mix dry ingredients into wet ingredients 1 cup at a time to make a smooth batter.

4. Ladle 1/2 cup batter, or amount recommended by manufacturer, into preheated waffle iron; close lid and cook waffle until crisp and browned, 3 to 5 minutes. Repeat with remaining batter.

Nutrition:

Calories: 313 calories Total Fat: 15.9 g Cholesterol: 64 mg Sodium: 506 mg Total Carbohydrate: 33.4 g Protein: 11.8 g

Whole Wheat Pecan Chaffles

Serving: 8

Preparation Time: 10 minutes Cooking Time: 20 minutes

Ingredients

- 2 cups whole wheat pastry flour

- 2 tablespoons sugar

- 3 teaspoons baking powder

- 1/2 teaspoon salt

- 1/2 cup mozzarella cheese, shredded
- 2 large eggs, separated

- 1-3/4 cups fat-free milk

- 1/4 cup canola oil

- 1/2 cup chopped pecans

Direction

1. Preheat waffle maker. Whisk together first four ingredients. In another bowl, whisk together egg yolks, milk and oil; add to flour mixture, stirring just until moistened. In a clean bowl, beat egg whites on medium speed until stiff but not dry. Add mozzarella cheese and stir well.

2. Fold into batter. Bake chaffles according to manufacturer's directions until golden brown, sprinkling batter with pecans after pouring. Freeze option: Cool chaffles on wire racks. Freeze between layers of waxed paper in a resealable plastic freezer bag. Reheat chaffles in a toaster or toaster oven on medium setting.

Nutrition: Calories: 241 calories Total Fat: 14g Cholesterol: 48mg Sodium: 338mg Total Carbohydrate: 24g Protein: 7g Fiber: 3g

Chaffle Cannoli

Preparation Time: 15 minutes Cooking Time: 28 minutes Servings: 4

Ingredients:

For the chaffles:

- 1 large egg

- 1 egg yolk

- 3 tbsp butter, melted

- 1 tbso swerve confectioner's

- 1 cup finely grated Parmesan cheese

- 2 tbsp finely grated mozzarella cheese

For the cannoli filling:

- ½ cup ricotta cheese

- 2 tbsp swerve confectioner's sugar

- 1 tsp vanilla extract

- 2 tbsp unsweetened chocolate chips for garnishing

Directions:

1. Preheat the waffle iron.

2. Meanwhile, in a medium bowl, mix all the ingredients for the chaffles.

3. Open the iron, pour in a quarter of the mixture, cover, and cook until crispy, 7 minutes.

4. Remove the chaffle onto a plate and make 3 more with the remaining batter.

5. Meanwhile, for the cannoli filling:

6. Beat the ricotta cheese and swerve confectioner's sugar until smooth. Mix in the vanilla.

7. On each chaffle, spread some of the filling and wrap over.

8. Garnish the creamy ends with some chocolate chips.

9. Serve immediately.

Nutrition: Calories 308 Fats 25.05g Carbs 5.17g Net Carbs 5.17g Protein 15.18g

Keto Belgian Sugar Chaffles

Preparation Time: 10 minutes Cooking Time: 24 minutes Servings: 4

Ingredients:

- 1 egg, beaten

- 2 tbsp swerve brown sugar

- ½ tbsp butter, melted

- 1 tsp vanilla extract

- 1 cup finely grated Parmesan cheese

Directions:

1. Preheat the waffle iron.

2. Mix all the ingredients in a
   medium bowl.

3. Open the iron and pour in a quarter of
   the mixture. Close and cook until crispy,
   6 minutes.

4. Remove the chaffle onto a plate and
   make 3 more with the remaining
   ingredients.

5. Cut each chaffle into wedges, plate, allow
   cooling and serve.

Nutrition: Calories 136 Fats 9.45g Carbs 3.69g Net
Carbs 3.69g Protein 8.5g

Nutter Butter Chaffles

Preparation Time: 15 minutes Cooking Time: 14 minutes Servings: 2

Ingredients:

For the chaffles:

- 2 tbsp sugar-free peanut butter powder

- 2 tbsp maple (sugar-free) syrup

- 1 egg, beaten

- ¼ cup finely grated mozzarella cheese

- ¼ tsp baking powder

- ¼ tsp almond butter

- ¼ tsp peanut butter extract

- 1 tbsp softened cream cheese

For the frosting:

- ½ cup almond flour

- 1 cup peanut butter

- 3 tbsp almond milk

- ½ tsp vanilla extract

- ½ cup maple (sugar-free) syrup

Directions:

6. Preheat the waffle iron.

7. Meanwhile, in a medium bowl, mix all the ingredients until smooth.

8. Open the iron and pour in half of the mixture.

9. Close the iron and cook until crispy, 6 to 7 minutes.

10. Remove the chaffle onto a plate and set aside.

11. Make a second chaffle with the remaining batter.

12. While the chaffles cool, make the frosting.

13. Pour the almond flour in a medium saucepan and stir-fry over medium heat until golden.

14. Transfer the almond flour to a blender and top with the remaining frosting ingredients. Process until smooth.

15. 1Spread the frosting on the chaffles and serve afterward.

Nutrition: Calories 239 Fats 15.48g Carbs 17.42g Net Carbs 15.92g Protein 7.52g

Chaffled Brownie Sundae

Preparation Time: 12 minutes Cooking Time: 30 minutes Servings: 4

Ingredients:

For the chaffles:

- 2 eggs, beaten

- 1 tbsp unsweetened cocoa powder

- 1 tbsp erythritol

- 1 cup finely grated mozzarella cheese

For the topping:

- 3 tbsp unsweetened chocolate, chopped

- 3 tbsp unsalted butter

- ½ cup swerve sugar

- Low-carb ice cream for topping

- 1 cup whipped cream for topping

- 3 tbsp sugar-free caramel sauce

Directions:

For the chaffles:

16. Preheat the waffle iron.

17. Meanwhile, in a medium bowl, mix all the ingredients for the chaffles.

18. Open the iron, pour in a quarter of the mixture, cover, and cook until crispy, 7 minutes.

19. Remove the chaffle onto a plate and make 3 more with the remaining batter.

20. Plate and set aside.

For the topping:

Meanwhile, melt the chocolate and butter in a medium saucepan with

occasional stirring, 2 minutes.

To Servings:

1. Divide the chaffles into wedges and top with the ice cream, whipped cream, and swirl the chocolate sauce and caramel sauce on top.

2. Serve immediately.

Nutrition: Calories 165 Fats 11.39g Carbs 3.81g Net Carbs 2.91g Protein 12.79g

Brie and Blackberry Chaffles

Preparation Time: 15 minutes Cooking Time: 36 minutes Servings: 4

Ingredients:

For the chaffles:

- 2 eggs, beaten

- 1 cup finely grated mozzarella cheese

For the topping:

- 1 ½ cups blackberries

- 1 lemon, 1 tsp zest and 2 tbsp juice

- 1 tbsp erythritol

- 4 slices Brie cheese

Directions:

For the chaffles:

1. Preheat the waffle iron.

2. Meanwhile, in a medium bowl, mix the eggs and mozzarella cheese.

3. Open the iron, pour in a quarter of the mixture, cover, and cook until crispy, 7

minutes.

4. Remove the chaffle onto a plate and make 3 more with the remaining batter.

5. Plate and set aside.

For the topping:

1. Preheat the oven to 350 F and line a baking sheet with parchment paper.

2. In a medium pot, add the blackberries, lemon zest, lemon juice, and erythritol. Cook until the blackberries break and the sauce thickens, 5 minutes. Turn the heat off.

3. Arrange the chaffles on the baking sheet and place two Brie cheese slices on each. Top with blackberry mixture and transfer the baking sheet to the oven.

4. Bake until the cheese melts, 2 to 3 minutes.

5. Remove from the oven, allow cooling and serve afterward.

Nutrition: Calories 576 Fats 42.22g Carbs 7.07g Net Carbs 3.67g Protein 42.35g

Cereal Chaffle Cake

Preparation Time: 5 minutes Cooking
Time: 8 minutes Servings: 2

Ingredients:

- 1 egg

- 2 tablespoons almond flour

- ½ teaspoon coconut flour

- 1 tablespoon melted butter

- 1 tablespoon cream cheese

- 1 tablespoon plain cereal, crushed
    - ¼ teaspoon vanilla extract

    - ¼ teaspoon baking powder

    - 1 tablespoon sweetener

    - 1/8 teaspoon xanthan gum

Directions:

1. Plug in your waffle maker to preheat.

2. Add all the ingredients in a large bowl.

3. Mix until well blended.

4. Let the batter rest for 2 minutes before cooking.

5. Pour half of the mixture into the waffle maker.

6. Seal and cook for 4 minutes.

7. Make the next chaffle using the same steps.

Nutrition:

Calories154

Total Fat 21.2g Saturated Fat 10 g Cholesterol 113.3mg Sodium 96.9mg Potassium 453 mg Total Carbohydrate 5.9g Dietary Fiber 1.7g Protein 4.6g Total Sugars 2.7g

Ham, Cheese & Tomato Chaffle Sandwich

Preparation Time: 5 minutes Cooking
Time: 10 minutes Servings: 2

Ingredients:

- 1 teaspoon olive oil

- 2 slices ham

- 4 basic chaffles

- 1 tablespoon mayonnaise

- 2 slices Provolone cheese

- 1 tomato, sliced

Directions:

1. Add the olive oil to a pan over medium heat.
2. Cook the ham for 1 minute per side.
3. Spread the chaffles with mayonnaise.
4. Top with the ham, cheese and tomatoes.
5. Top with another chaffle to make a sandwich.

Nutrition:

Calories 198

Total Fat 14.7g Saturated Fat 6.3g Cholesterol 37mg Sodium 664mg Total Carbohydrate 4.6g Dietary Fiber 0.7g Total Sugars 1.5g Protein 12.2g Potassium 193mg

Barbecue Chaffle

Preparation Time: 5 minutes
Cooking Time: 8 minutes Servings: 2

Ingredients:

- 1 egg, beaten

- ½ cup cheddar cheese, shredded

- ½ teaspoon barbecue sauce

- ¼ teaspoon baking powder

Directions:

1. Plug in your waffle maker to preheat.

2. Mix all the ingredients in a bowl.

3. Pour half of the mixture to your waffle maker.

4. Cover and cook for 4 minutes.

5. Repeat the same steps for the next barbecue chaffle.

Nutrition: Calories 295 Total Fat 23 g Saturated Fat 13 g Cholesterol 223 mg Sodium 414 mg Potassium 179 mg Total Carbohydrate 2 g Dietary Fiber 1 g Protein 20 g Total Sugars 1 g

Ranch Chaffle

Preparation Time: 5 minutes Cooking Time:
8 minutes Servings: 2

Ingredients:

- 1 egg

- ¼ cup chicken cubes, cooked

- 1 slice bacon, cooked and chopped

- ¼ cup cheddar cheese, shredded

- 1 teaspoon ranch dressing powder

Directions:

1. Preheat your waffle maker.
2. In a bowl, mix all the
   ingredients.

3. Add half of the mixture to your waffle
   maker.

4. Cover and cook for 4 minutes.

5. Make the second chaffle using the same
   steps.

Nutrition: Calories 200 Total Fat 14 g Saturated Fat 6 g Cholesterol 129 mg Sodium 463 mg Potassium 130 mg Total Carbohydrate 2 g Dietary Fiber 1 g Protein 16 g Total Sugars 1 g

Cream Cheese Chaffle

Preparation Time: 5 minutes Cooking
Time: 8 minutes Servings: 2

Ingredients:

- 1 egg, beaten

- 1 oz. cream cheese

- ½ teaspoon vanilla

- 4 teaspoons sweetener

- ¼ teaspoon baking powder

- Cream cheese

Directions:

1. Preheat your waffle maker.

2. Add all the ingredients in a bowl.

3. Mix well.

4. Pour half of the batter into the waffle maker.

5. Seal the device.

6. Cook for 4 minutes.

7. Remove the chaffle from the waffle maker.

8. Make the second one using the same steps.

9. Spread remaining cream cheese on top before serving.

Nutrition: Calories 169 Total Fat 14.3g Saturated Fat 7.6g Cholesterol 195mg Sodium 147mg Potassium 222mg Total Carbohydrate 4g Dietary Fiber 4g Protein 7.7g Total Sugars 0.7g

Creamy Chicken Chaffle Sandwich

Preparation Time: 5 minutes Cooking Time: 10 minutes Servings: 2

Ingredients:

- Cooking spray

- 1 cup chicken breast fillet, cubed

- Salt and pepper to taste

- ¼ cup all-purpose cream

- 4 garlic chaffles
    - Parsley, chopped

Directions:

1. Spray your pan with oil.

2. Put it over medium heat.

3. Add the chicken fillet cubes.

4. Season with salt and pepper.

5. Reduce heat and add the cream.

6. Spread chicken mixture on top of the chaffle.

7. Garnish with parsley and top with another chaffle.

Nutrition: Calories 273 Total Fat 38.4g Saturated Fat 4.1g Cholesterol 62mg Sodium 373mg Total Carbohydrate 22.5g Dietary Fiber 1.1g Total Sugars 3.2g Protein 17.5g Potassium 177mg

Turkey Chaffle Burger

Preparation Time: 10 minutes Cooking
Time: 10 minutes Servings: 2

Ingredients:

- 2 cups ground turkey

- Salt and pepper to taste

- 1 tablespoon olive oil

- 4 garlic chaffles

- 1 cup Romaine lettuce, chopped

- 1 tomato, sliced

- Mayonnaise

- Ketchup

Directions:

1. Combine ground turkey, salt and pepper. Form 2 thick burger patties.

2. Add the olive oil to a pan over medium heat.

3. Cook the turkey burger until fully cooked on both sides.

4. Spread mayo on the chaffle.

5. Top with the turkey burger, lettuce and tomato.

6. Squirt ketchup on top before topping with another chaffle.

Nutrition: Calories 555 Total Fat 21.5g Saturated Fat 3.5g Cholesterol 117mg Sodium 654mg Total Carbohydrate 4.1g Dietary Fiber 2.5g Protein 31.7g Total Sugars 1g

Savory Beef Chaffle

Preparation Time: 10 minutes
Cooking Time: 15 minutes Servings: 2

Ingredients:

- 1 teaspoon olive oil

- 2 cups ground beef

- Garlic salt to taste

- 1 red bell pepper, sliced into strips

- 1 green bell pepper, sliced into strips

- 1 onion, minced

- 1 bay leaf

- 2 garlic chaffles

- Butter

Directions:

1. Put your pan over medium heat.

2. Add the olive oil and cook ground beef until brown.

3. Season with garlic salt and add bay leaf.

4. Drain the fat, transfer to a plate and set aside.

   5. Discard the bay leaf.

   6. In the same pan, cook the onion and bell peppers for 2 minutes.

   7. Put the beef back to the pan.

   8. Heat for 1 minute.

   9. Spread butter on top of the chaffle.

   10. 1Add the ground beef and veggies.

   11. 1Roll or fold the chaffle.

Nutrition: Calories 220 Total Fat 17.8g Saturated Fat 8g Cholesterol 76mg Sodium 60mg Total Carbohydrate 3g Dietary Fiber 2g Total Sugars 5.4g Protein 27.1g Potassium 537mg

Bruschetta Chaffle

Preparation Time: 5 minutes Cooking
Time: 5 minutes Servings: 2

Ingredients:

- 2 basic chaffles

- 2 tablespoons sugar-free marinara
  sauce

- 2 tablespoons mozzarella, shredded

- 1 tablespoon olives, sliced

- 1 tomato sliced

- 1 tablespoon keto friendly pesto
  sauce

- Basil leaves

Directions:

1. Spread marinara sauce on each
   chaffle.

2. Spoon pesto and spread on top of the
   marinara sauce.

3. Top with the tomato, olives and

mozzarella.

4. Bake in the oven for 3 minutes or until the cheese has melted.

5. Garnish with basil.

6. Serve and enjoy.

Nutrition: Calories 182 Total Fat 11g Saturated Fat 6.1g Cholesterol 30mg Sodium 508mg Potassium 1mg Total Carbohydrate 3.1g Dietary Fiber 1.1g Protein 16.8g Total Sugars 1g

Asian Cauliflower Chaffles

Preparation Time: 20 minutes Cooking Time: 28 minutes Servings: 4

Ingredients:

For the chaffles:

- 1 cup cauliflower rice, steamed

- 1 large egg, beaten

- Salt and freshly ground black pepper to taste
- 1 cup finely grated Parmesan cheese

- 1 tsp sesame seeds

- ¼ cup chopped fresh scallions

For the dipping sauce:

- 3 tbsp coconut aminos

- 1 ½ tbsp plain vinegar

- 1 tsp fresh ginger puree

- 1 tsp fresh garlic paste

- 3 tbsp sesame oil

- 1 tsp fish sauce

- 1 tsp red chili flakes

Directions:

1. Preheat the waffle iron.

2. In a medium bowl, mix the cauliflower rice, egg, salt, black pepper, and Parmesan cheese.

3. Open the iron and add a quarter of the mixture. Close and cook until crispy, 7 minutes.

4. Transfer the chaffle to a plate and make 3 more chaffles in the same manner.

5. Meanwhile, make the dipping sauce.

6. In a medium bowl, mix all the ingredients for the dipping sauce.

7. Plate the chaffles, garnish with the sesame seeds and scallions and serve with the dipping sauce.

Nutrition: Calories 231 Fats 18.88g Carbs 6.32g Net Carbs 5.42g Protein 9.66g

Hot Dog Chaffles

Preparation Time: 15 minutes Cooking Time: 14 minutes Servings: 2

Ingredients:

- 1 egg, beaten

- 1 cup finely grated cheddar cheese

- 2 hot dog sausages, cooked

- Mustard dressing for topping

- 8 pickle slices

Directions:

1. Preheat the waffle iron.

2. In a medium bowl, mix the egg and cheddar cheese.

3. Open the iron and add half of the mixture. Close and cook until crispy, 7 minutes.

4. Transfer the chaffle to a plate and make a second chaffle in the same manner.

5. To serve, top each chaffle with a sausage, swirl the mustard dressing on

top, and then divide the pickle slices on top.

6. Enjoy!

Nutrition: Calories 231 Fats 18.29g Carbs 2.8g Net Carbs 2.6g Protein 13.39g

Turnip Hash Brown Chaffles

Preparation Time: 10 minutes Cooking Time: 42 minutes Servings: 6

Ingredients:

- 1 large turnip, peeled and shredded

- ½ medium white onion, minced

- 2 garlic cloves, pressed

- 1 cup finely grated Gouda cheese
- 2 eggs, beaten

- Salt and freshly ground black pepper to taste

Directions:

1. Pour the turnips in a medium safe microwave bowl, sprinkle with 1 tbsp of water, and steam in the microwave until softened, 1 to 2 minutes.

2. Remove the bowl and mix in the remaining ingredients except for a quarter cup of the Gouda cheese.

3. Preheat the waffle iron.

4. Once heated, open and sprinkle some of the reserved cheese in the iron and top with 3 tablespoons of the mixture. Close the waffle iron and cook until crispy, 5 minutes.

5. Open the lid, flip the chaffle and cook further for 2 more minutes.

6. Remove the chaffle onto a plate and set aside.

7. Make five more chaffles with the remaining batter in the same proportion.

8. Allow cooling and serve afterward.

Nutrition: Calories 230; Fats 15.85g; Carbs 5.01g; Net Carbs 3.51g; Protein 16.57g

Savory Gruyere and Chives Chaffles

Preparation Time: 15 minutes Cooking Time: 14 minutes Servings: 2

Ingredients:

- 2 eggs, beaten

- 1 cup finely grated Gruyere cheese
- 2 tbsp finely grated cheddar cheese

- 1/8 tsp freshly ground black pepper

- 3 tbsp minced fresh chives + more for garnishing

- 2 sunshine fried eggs for topping

Directions:

1. Preheat the waffle iron.

2. In a medium bowl, mix the eggs, cheeses, black pepper, and chives.

3. Open the iron and pour in half of the mixture.

4. Close the iron and cook until brown and

crispy, 7 minutes.

5. Remove the chaffle onto a plate and
   set aside.

6. Make another chaffle using the
   remaining mixture.

7. Top each chaffle with one fried egg
   each, garnish with the chives and serve.

Nutrition: Calories 712 Fats 41.32g Carbs 3.88g
Net Carbs 3.78g Protein
23.75g

Maple Chaffle

Preparation Time: 15 minutes Servings: 2

Ingredients:

- 1 egg, lightly beaten

- 2 egg whites

- 1/2 tsp maple extract

- 2 tsp Swerve

- 1/2 tsp baking powder, gluten-free

- 2 tbsp almond milk

- 2 tbsp coconut flour

Directions:

1. Preheat your waffle maker.

2. In a bowl, whip egg whites until stiff peaks form.

3. Stir in maple extract, Swerve, baking powder, almond milk, coconut flour, and egg.

4. Spray waffle maker with cooking spray.

5. Pour half batter in the hot waffle maker and cook for 3-5 minutes or until golden brown. Repeat with the remaining batter.

6. Serve and enjoy.

Nutrition: Calories 122 Fat 6.6 g Carbohydrates 9 g Sugar 1 g Protein 7.8 g Cholesterol 82 mg

Keto Chocolate Fudge Chaffle

Preparation Time: 10 minutes Cooking Time: 14 minutes Servings: 2

Ingredients:

- 1 egg, beaten

- ¼ cup finely grated Gruyere cheese

- 2 tbsp unsweetened cocoa powder

- ¼ tsp baking powder
- ¼ tsp vanilla extract

- 2 tbsp erythritol

- 1 tsp almond flour

- 1 tsp heavy whipping cream

- A pinch of salt

Directions:

1. Preheat the waffle iron.

2. Add all the ingredients to a medium bowl and mix well.

3. Open the iron and add half of the mixture. Close and cook until golden brown and crispy, 7 minutes.

4. Remove the chaffle onto a plate and make another with the remaining batter.

5. Cut each chaffle into wedges and serve after.

Nutrition: Calories 173 Fats 13.08g Carbs 3.98g Net Carbs 2.28g Protein 12.27g

Blue Cheese Chaffle Bites

Preparation Time: 10 minutes Cooking Time: 14 minutes Servings: 2

Ingredients:

- 1 egg, beaten

- ½ cup finely grated Parmesan cheese

- ¼ cup crumbled blue cheese

- 1 tsp erythritol

Directions:

1. Preheat the waffle iron.

2. Mix all the ingredients in a bowl.

3. Open the iron and add half of the mixture. Close and cook until crispy, 7 minutes.

4. Remove the chaffle onto a plate and make another with the remaining mixture.

5. Cut each chaffle into wedges and serve afterward.

Nutrition: Calories 196 Fats 13.91g Carbs 4.03g Net Carbs 4.03g Protein 13.48g

Lemon and Paprika Chaffles

Preparation Time: 10 minutes Cooking
Time: 28 minutes Servings: 4

Ingredients:

- 1 egg, beaten

- 1 oz cream cheese, softened

- 1/3 cup finely grated mozzarella
  cheese

- 1 tbsp almond flour

- 1 tsp butter, melted

- 1 tsp maple (sugar-free) syrup

- ½ tsp sweet paprika

- ½ tsp lemon extract

Directions:

1. Preheat the waffle iron.

2. Mix all the ingredients in a medium bowl

3. Open the iron and pour in a quarter of the mixture. Close and cook until crispy, 7 minutes.

4. Remove the chaffle onto a plate and make 3 more with the remaining mixture.

5. Cut each chaffle into wedges, plate, allow cooling and serve.

Nutrition: Calories 48 Fats 4.22g Carbs 0.6g Net Carbs 0.5g Protein 2g

Breakfast Spinach Ricotta Chaffles

Preparation Time: 10 minutes Cooking
Time: 28 minutes Servings: 4

Ingredients:

- 4 oz frozen spinach, thawed, squeezed
  dry

- 1 cup ricotta cheese

- 2 eggs, beaten

- ½ tsp garlic powder
- ¼ cup finely grated Pecorino Romano cheese

- ½ cup finely grated mozzarella cheese

- Salt and freshly ground black pepper to taste

Directions:

1. Preheat the waffle iron.

2. In a medium bowl, mix all the ingredients.

3. Open the iron, lightly grease with cooking spray and spoon in a quarter of the mixture.

4. Close the iron and cook until brown and crispy, 7 minutes.

5. Remove the chaffle onto a plate and set aside.

6. Make three more chaffles with the remaining mixture.

7. Allow cooling and serve afterward.

Nutrition: Calories 188 Fats 13.15g Carbs 5.06g Net Carbs 4.06g Protein 12.79g

Scrambled Egg Stuffed Chaffles

Preparation Time: 15 minutes Cooking
Time: 28 minutes Servings: 4

Ingredients:

For the chaffles:

- 1 cup finely grated cheddar cheese

- 2 eggs, beaten

For the egg stuffing:

- 1 tbsp olive oil

- 4 large eggs

- 1 small green bell pepper, deseeded
  and chopped

- 1 small red bell pepper, deseeded
  and chopped

- Salt and freshly ground black pepper to
  taste

- 2 tbsp grated Parmesan cheese

Directions:

For the chaffles:

1. Preheat the waffle iron.

2. In a medium bowl, mix the cheddar cheese and egg.

3. Open the iron, pour in a quarter of the mixture, close, and cook until crispy, 6 to 7 minutes.

4. Plate and make three more chaffles using the remaining mixture.

For the egg stuffing:

1. Meanwhile, heat the olive oil in a medium skillet over medium heat on a stovetop.

2. In a medium bowl, beat the eggs with the bell peppers, salt, black pepper, and Parmesan cheese.

3. Pour the mixture into the skillet and scramble until set to your likeness, 2 minutes.

4. Between two chaffles, spoon half of the scrambled eggs and repeat with the second set of chaffles.

5. Serve afterward.

Nutrition: Calories 387 Fats 22.52g Carbs 18.12g Net Carbs 17.52g Protein 27.76g

Mixed Berry- Vanilla Chaffles

Preparation Time: 10 minutes Cooking Time: 28 minutes Servings: 4

Ingredients:

- 1 egg, beaten

- ½ cup finely grated mozzarella cheese

- 1 tbsp cream cheese, softened

- 1 tbsp sugar-free maple syrup

- 2 strawberries, sliced
- 2 raspberries, slices

- ¼ tsp blackberry extract

- ¼ tsp vanilla extract

- ½ cup plain yogurt for serving

Directions:

1. Preheat the waffle iron.

2. In a medium bowl, mix all the ingredients except the yogurt.

3. Open the iron, lightly grease with cooking spray and pour in a quarter of the mixture.

4. Close the iron and cook until golden brown and crispy, 7 minutes.

5. Remove the chaffle onto a plate and set aside.

6. Make three more chaffles with the remaining mixture.

7. To Servings: top with the yogurt and enjoy.

Nutrition: Calories 78 Fats 5.29g Carbs 3.02g Net Carbs 2.72g Protein 4.32g

Chaffles with Vanilla Sauce

Serving: 6-8 chaffles (6-1/2 inches).

Preparation Time: 15 minutes Cooking
Time: 30 minutes

Ingredients

- 1-2/3 cups all-purpose flour

- 4 teaspoons baking powder

- 1/2 teaspoon salt

- 2 eggs, separated

- 3-2/3 cups milk, divided

- 6 tablespoons canola oil

- 1/2 cup sugar

- 1 teaspoon vanilla extract

- 1/2 cup mozzarella cheese, shredded

- Fresh strawberries

Direction

1. In a bowl, combine flour, baking
    powder and salt. In another bowl, beat
    egg yolks lightly. Add 1-2/3 cups milk
    and oil; stir into dry

    ingredients just until moistened. Set aside 1/4
    cup batter in a small bowl. Beat egg whites
    until stiff peaks form; fold into remaining
    batter. Add mozzarella cheese and stir well.

2. Bake in a preheated waffle iron according to
    manufacturer's directions until golden brown.
    In a saucepan, heat sugar and remaining milk
    until scalded. Stir a small amount into
    reserved batter; return all to pan. Bring to a
    boil; boil for 5- 7 minutes or until thickened.
    Remove from the heat; add vanilla and mix
    well (sauce will thicken upon standing). Serve
    over chaffles. Top with berries.

**Nutrition: Calories: 429 calories Total Fat: 21g
Cholesterol: 91mg Sodium: 558mg Total
Carbohydrate: 50g Protein: 11g Fiber: 1g**

Pecan Pumpkin Chaffle

Preparation Time: 15 minutes Servings: 2

Ingredients:

- 1 egg

- 2 tbsp pecans, toasted and chopped

- 2 tbsp almond flour

- 1 tsp erythritol

- 1/4 tsp pumpkin pie spice

- 1 tbsp pumpkin puree

- 1/2 cup mozzarella cheese, grated

Directions:

1. Preheat your waffle maker.
2. Beat egg in a small bowl.
3. Add remaining ingredients and mix well.
4. Spray waffle maker with cooking spray.
5. Pour half batter in the hot waffle maker and cook for 5 minutes or until golden brown. Repeat with the remaining batter.
6. Serve and enjoy.

Nutrition: Calories 121 Fat 9.7 g
Carbohydrates 5.7 g Sugar 3.3 g
Protein 6.7 g Cholesterol 86 mg

Cinnamon Sugar Cupcakes

- 1.5 cups Almond Flour
- 1.5 tsp Baking Powder
- ¼ tsp Salt
- ½ tsp Cinnamon
- ½ cup Erythritol
- 1/3 cup Milk
- 2 large Whole Eggs
- 1 stick Butter, softened
- 2 tsp Lemon Zest

Preparation Time: 10 minutes

Cooking Time: 25 min   Servings:6

Nutritional Values:

- Fat: 29 g.
- Protein: 8 g.
- Carbs: 7 g.

Ingredients:

Directions:

1. Preheat oven to 350F.

2. Whisk together almond flour, baking powder, cinnamon, and salt in a bowl.

3. Beat eggs, butter, and erythritol in a separate bowl. Gradually stir in the milk.

4. Stir the wet mixture into the dry ingredients.

5. Coat a 6-hole muffin pan with non-stick spray.

6. Divide the batter into the pan and bake for 25 minutes.

Strawberry Cream Cheese Cupcakes

Ingredients:

- 1 cup Almond Flour
- 1 tsp Baking Powder
- ¼ tsp Salt
- ½ cup Erythritol
- 1/3 cup Milk
- 2 large Whole Eggs
- 1/3 cup Cream Cheese, softened
- 1 cup Frozen Strawberries, diced

Preparation Time: 10 minutes Cooking Time: 25 min

Servings:6

Nutritional Values:

- Fat: 14 g.
- Protein: 7 g.
- Carbs: 9 g.

Directions:

1. Preheat oven to 350F.

2. Whisk together almond flour, baking powder, and salt in a bowl.

3. Beat eggs, erythritol, and cream cheese in a separate bowl. Gradually stir in the milk.

4. Stir the wet mixture into the dry ingredients.

5. Fold in the strawberries.

6. Coat a 6-hole muffin pan with non-stick spray.

7. Divide the batter into the pan and bake for 25 minutes.

Coco-Blueberry Cupcakes

Preparation Time: 10 minutes

Cooking Time: 25 min Servings:6

Nutritional Values:

- Fat: 30 g.
- Protein: 6 g.
- Carbs: 7 g.

Ingredients:

- 1 cup Almond Flour
- 1/2 cup Coconut Flour
- 1 tbsp Flax Meal
- 1 tsp Baking Powder
- ¼ tsp Salt
- ½ cup Erythritol
- 1/3 cup Milk
- 2 large Whole Eggs
- ½ cup Frozen Blueberries
- ½ cup Coconut Oil

Directions:

1. Preheat oven to 350F.

2. Whisk together almond flour, coconut flour, baking powder, and salt in a bowl.

3. Beat eggs, coconut oil, and erythritol in a separate bowl.
   Gradually stir in the milk.

4. Stir the wet mixture into the dry ingredients.

   5. Fold in the blueberries.

   6. Coat a 6-hole muffin pan with non-stick spray.

   7. Divide the batter into the pan and bake for 25
      minutes.

Choco-Hazelnut Cupcakes

Preparation Time: 10 minutes

Cooking Time: 25 min Servings:6

Nutritional Values:

- Fat: 29 g.
- Protein: 9 g.
- Carbs: 9 g.

- 1.25 cup Almond Flour
- ¼ cup Unsweetened Cocoa Powder
- 1.5 tsp Baking Powder
- ¼ tsp Salt
- ½ cup Erythritol
- 1/3 cup Milk
- 2 large Whole Eggs
- 1 tsp Vanilla Extract
- 1/3 cup Hazelnut Butter
- ½ cup Sugar-Free Chocolate Chips
- ½ cup Hazelnuts, chopped

Directions:

1. Preheat oven to 350F.

2. Whisk together almond flour, cocoa powder, baking powder, and salt in a bowl.

3. Beat eggs, hazelnut butter, vanilla, and erythritol in a separate bowl. Gradually stir in the milk.

4. Stir the wet mixture into the dry ingredients.

5. Fold in the chocolate chips and hazelnuts.

6. Coat a 6-hole muffin pan with non-stick spray.

7. Divide the batter into the pan and bake for 25 minutes.

Cheddar and Spinach Cupcakes

Preparation Time: 10 minutes Cooking Time: 25 min

Servings:6

Nutritional Values:

Fat: 17 g.
Protein: 9 g.
Carbs: 5 g.

Ingredients:

- 1 cup Almond Flour
- 1 tsp Baking Powder
- ¼ tsp Salt
- ½ cup Erythritol
- 1/3 cup Milk
- 2 large Whole Eggs
- 1/3 cup Cream Cheese, softened
- ½ cup Cheddar, shredded
- 1/3 cup Frozen Spinach, thawed and chopped

Directions:

1. Preheat oven to 350F.

2. Whisk together almond flour, baking powder, and salt in a bowl.

3. Beat eggs, cream cheese, and erythritol in a separate bowl. Gradually stir in the milk.

4. Stir the wet mixture into the dry ingredients.

5. Fold in the cheddar and spinach.

6. Coat a 6-hole muffin pan with non-stick spray.

7. Divide the batter into the pan and bake for 25 minutes.

Mango-Cayenne Cupcakes

Preparation Time: 10 minutes Cooking Time: 25 min

Servings:6

Nutritional Values:

> Fat: 25 g.
> Protein: 8 g.
> Carbs: 7 g.

Ingredients:

- 1 cup Almond Flour
- 1/2 cup Coconut Flour
- 1 tbsp Flax Meal
- ½ tsp Cayenne
- 1 tsp Baking Powder
- ¼ tsp Salt
- ½ cup Erythritol
- 1/3 cup Milk
- 2 large Whole Eggs
- ½ cup Sugar-Free Mango Jelly
- ½ cup Butter, softened

Directions:

1. Preheat oven to 350F.

2. Whisk together almond flour, coconut flour, baking powder, flax meal, cayenne, and salt in a bowl.

3. Beat eggs, mango jelly, butter, and erythritol in a separate bowl. Gradually stir in the milk.

4. Stir the wet mixture into the dry ingredients.

5. Coat a 6-hole muffin pan with non-stick spray.

6. Divide the batter into the pan and bake for 25 minutes.

Lime and Vanilla Cupcakes

Preparation Time: 10

minutes Cooking Time: 25

min Servings:6

Nutritional Values:

- Fat: 29 g.
- Protein: 8 g.
- Carbs: 7 g.

Ingredients:

- 1.5 cups Almond Flour
- 1.5 tsp Baking Powder
- ¼ tsp Salt
- ½ cup Erythritol
- 1/3 cup Milk
- 2 large Whole Eggs
- 1 tsp Vanilla Extract
- 1 stick Butter, softened
- 2 tsp Lime Zest

Directions:

1. Preheat oven to 350F.
2. Whisk together almond flour, baking powder, and salt in a bowl.
3. Beat eggs, butter, and erythritol, and vanilla in a separate bowl. Gradually stir in the milk.
4. Stir the wet mixture into the dry ingredients.
5. Fold in the lime zest.
6. Coat a 6-hole muffin pan with non-stick spray.
7. Divide the batter into the pan and bake for 25 minutes.

Chia Chocolate Cupcakes

Ingredients:

- 1.25 cup Almond Flour¼ cup Unsweetened Cocoa Powder
- 1.5 tsp Baking Powder
- ¼ tsp Salt
- ½ cup Erythritol
- 1/3 cup Milk
- 2 large Whole Eggs
- 1 tsp Vanilla Extract
- ½ cup Butter
- ½ cup Sugar-Free Chocolate Chips
- 2 tbsp Chia Seeds
-

Directions:

1. Preheat oven to 350F.
2. Whisk together almond flour, cocoa powder, baking powder, and salt in a bowl.
3. Beat eggs, butter, vanilla, and erythritol in a separate bowl. Gradually stir in the milk.
4. Stir the wet mixture into the dry ingredients.
5. Fold in the chocolate chips and chia seeds.
6. Coat a 6-hole muffin pan with non-stick spray.
7. Divide the batter into the pan and bake for 25 minutes.

Cooking Time: 25 min   Servings:6

Nutritional Values:

- Fat: 23 g.
- Protein: 8 g.
- Carbs: 8 g.

Keto Cheese Bread

•

Ingredients:

- 1 cup Almond Flour
- 1 tsp Baking Powder
- ¼ tsp Salt
- 1/3 cup Milk
- 2 large Whole Eggs
- 1/3 cup Cream Cheese, softened
- ½ cup Grated Parmesan

Preparation Time: 10

minutes Cooking Time: 25

min Servings:6

Nutritional Values:

- Fat: 16 g.
- Protein: 9 g.
- Carbs: 6 g.

Directions:

1. Preheat oven to 350F.

2. Whisk together almond flour, baking powder, and salt in a bowl.

3. Beat eggs and cream cheese in a separate bowl. Gradually stir in the milk.

4. Stir the wet mixture into the dry ingredients.

5. Fold in the grated parmesan.

6. Coat a 6-hole muffin tin with non-stick spray.

7. Divide the batter into the pan and bake for 25 minutes.

Keto Mug Bread

Preparation Time: 2

min Cooking Time: 2

min Servings:1

Nutritional Values:

- Fat: 37 g.
- Protein: 15 g.
- Carbs: 8 g.

Ingredients:

- 1/3 cup Almond Flour
- ½ tsp Baking Powder
    - ¼ tsp Salt
    - 1 Whole Egg
    - 1 tbsp Melted Butter

Directions:

1. Mix all ingredients in a microwave-safe mug.
2. Microwave for 90 seconds.
3. Cool for 2 minutes.

Keto Blender Buns

Nutritional Values:

- Fat: 18 g.
- Protein: 8 g.
- Carbs: 2 g.

Ingredients:

- 4 Whole Eggs
- ¼ cup Melted Butter
- ½ tsp Salt
- ½ cup Almond Flour
- 1 tsp Italian Spice Mix

<u>Directions:</u>

1. Preheat oven to 425F.

2. Pulse all ingredients in a blender.

3. Divide batter into a 6-hole muffin tin.

4. Bake for 25 minutes.

Keto Ciabatta

- 1 cup Almond Flour

Preparation Time: 1 hour

Cooking Time: 30 minutes   Servings:8

Nutritional Values:

- Fat: 11 g.
- Protein: 3 g.
- Carbs: 4 g.
- ¼ cup Psyllium Husk Powder
- ½ tsp Salt
- 1 tsp Baking Powder
- 3 tbsp Olive Oil
- 1 tsp Maple Syrup
- 1 tbsp Active Dry Yeast
- 1 cup Warm Water
- 1 tbsp Chopped Rosemary

Directions:

1. In a bowl, stir together warm water, maple syrup, and yeast. Leave for 10 minutes.

2. In a separate bowl, whisk together almond flour, psyllium husk powder, salt, chopped rosemary, and baking powder.

3. Stir in the olive oil and yeast mixture into the dry ingredients until a smooth dough is formed.

4. Knead the dough until smooth.

5. Divide the dough into 2 and shape into buns.

6. Set both buns on a baking sheet lined with parchment. Leave to rise for an hour.

7. Bake for 30 minutes at 380F.

1.

Chocolate Muffins

Serving: 10 muffins

Serving: 10 muffins Nutritional Values: Calories:

168.8,

Total Fat: 13.2 g, Saturated Fat: 1.9 g, Carbs: 19.6 g,

Sugars: 0.7 g,

Protein: 6.1 g

- Ingredients:
- 2 tsp Cream of Tartar
- 1/2 cup Erythritol
- 1 tsp Cinnamon
- Coconut Oil, for greasing

Wet ingredients:

- 2 oz medium Avocados, peeled and deseeded
- 4 Eggs
- 15-20 drops Stevia Drops
- 2 Tbsp Coconut Milk

Dry ingredients:

- 1 cup Almond Flour
- 1/3 cup Coconut Flour
- 1/2 cup Cocoa Powder
- 1 tsp Baking Soda

Directions:

1. Preheat your oven to 350F / 175C. Grease muffin cups with coconut oil and line your muffin tin.
2. Add the avocados to your food processor and pulse until smooth. Add the wet ingredients, pulse to combine until well incorporated.
3. Combine the dry ingredients and add to the food process and pulse to combine and pour the batter into your muffin tin.
4. Bake in the preheated oven for about 20-25 minutes.
5. Once crispy and baked, remove from the oven and leave to cool before serving.

Crackers with Flax Seeds

Ingredients:

- 2 tbsp flax seeds
- 1/3 cup milk
- 2 tbsp coconut oil
- 1 cup coconut flour
- ½ tsp baking powder
- 1 tsp erythritol

Prep time: 20 minutes

Nutritional Values:

- Cooking time: 20 minutes
- Servings: 10
- Calories 104
- Total carbs 10.8 g
- Protein 3 g
- Total fat 5.9 g

1. Combine flour with baking powder, erythritol and flax seeds.

2. Gradually add milk and oil and knead the dough.

3. Wrap the dough in plastic wrap and put in the fridge for 15 minutes.

4. Divide the dough into 2 parts and roll it out with a rolling pin about 0.1 inch thick.

5. Cut out triangles.

6. Line a baking sheet with parchment paper and place the crackers on it.

7. Bake at 390°F for 20 minutes.

Rye Crackers

- 1 cup rye flour
- 2/3 cup bran
- 2 tsp baking powder
- 3 tbsp vegetable oil
- 1 tsp liquid malt extract
- 1 tsp apple vinegar
- 1 cup water
- Salt to taste

Prep time: **10 minutes**

- Cooking time: 15 minutes
- Servings: 10

Nutritional Values:

- Calories 80
- Total carbs 10.4 g
- Protein 1.1 g
- Total fat 4.3 g

Directions:

1. Combine flour with bran, baking powder and salt.
2. Pour in oil, vinegar and malt extract. Mix well.
3. Knead the dough, gradually adding the water.
4. Divide the dough into 2 parts and roll it out with a rolling pin about 0.1 inch thick.
5. Cut out (using a knife or cookie cutter) the crackers of square or rectangle shape.
6. Line a baking sheet with parchment paper and place the crackers on it
7. Bake at 390°F for 12–15 minutes.

RECIPES

Beginners

Creamy Chicken Chaffle Sandwich

Preparation Time: 5 minutes
Cooking Time: 10 minutes
Servings: 2

Ingredients:

- Cooking spray
- 1 cup chicken breast fillet, cubed
- Salt and pepper to taste
- ¼ cup all-purpose cream
- 4 garlic chaffles
- Parsley, chopped

Directions:

1. Spray your pan with oil.
2. Put it over medium heat.
3. Add the chicken fillet cubes.
4. Season with salt and pepper.
5. Reduce heat and add the cream.
6. Spread chicken mixture on top of the chaffle.
7. Garnish with parsley and top with another chaffle.

Nutrition:

Calories 273
Total Fat 38.4g
Saturated Fat 4.1g
Cholesterol 62mg
Sodium 373mg
Total Carbohydrate 22.5g
Dietary Fiber 1.1g
Total Sugars 3.2g
Protein 17.5g
Potassium 177mg

Turkey Chaffle Burger

Preparation Time: 10 minutes
Cooking Time: 10 minutes
Servings: 2

Ingredients:

- 2 cups ground turkey
- Salt and pepper to taste
- 1 tablespoon olive oil
- 4 garlic chaffles
- 1 cup Romaine lettuce, chopped
- 1 tomato, sliced
- Mayonnaise
- Ketchup

Directions:

1. Combine ground turkey, salt and pepper.
2. Form 2 thick burger patties.
3. Add the olive oil to a pan over medium heat.
4. Cook the turkey burger until fully cooked on both sides.
5. Spread mayo on the chaffle.
6. Top with the turkey burger, lettuce and tomato.
7. Squirt ketchup on top before topping with another chaffle.

Nutrition:

Calories 555
Total Fat 21.5g
Saturated Fat 3.5g
Cholesterol 117mg
Sodium 654mg
Total Carbohydrate 4.1g
Dietary Fiber 2.5g
Protein 31.7g
Total Sugars 1g

Savory Beef Chaffle

Preparation Time: 10 minutes
Cooking Time: 15 minutes
Servings: 2

Ingredients:

- 1 teaspoon olive oil
- 2 cups ground beef
- Garlic salt to taste
- 1 red bell pepper, sliced into strips
- 1 green bell pepper, sliced into strips
- 1 onion, minced
- 1 bay leaf
- 2 garlic chaffles
- Butter

Directions:

1. Put your pan over medium heat.
2. Add the olive oil and cook ground beef until brown.
3. Season with garlic salt and add bay leaf.
4. Drain the fat, transfer to a plate and set aside.
5. Discard the bay leaf.
6. In the same pan, cook the onion and bell peppers for 2 minutes.
7. Put the beef back to the pan.
8. Heat for 1 minute.
9. Spread butter on top of the chaffle.
10. Add the ground beef and veggies.
11. Roll or fold the chaffle.

Nutrition:

Calories 220
Total Fat 17.8g
Saturated Fat 8g
Cholesterol 76mg
Sodium 60mg
Total Carbohydrate 3g
Dietary Fiber 2g
Total Sugars 5.4g
Protein 27.1g
Potassium 537mg

Egg & Chives Chaffle Sandwich Roll

Preparation Time: 5 minutes
Cooking Time: 0 minute
Servings: 2

Ingredients:

- 2 tablespoons mayonnaise
- 1 hard-boiled egg, chopped
- 1 tablespoon chives, chopped
- 2 basic chaffles

Directions:

1. In a bowl, mix the mayo, egg and chives.
2. Spread the mixture on top of the chaffles.
3. Roll the chaffle.

Nutrition:

Calories 258
Total Fat 14.2g
Saturated Fat 2.8g
Cholesterol 171mg
Sodium 271mg

Potassium 71mg
Total Carbohydrate 7.5g
Dietary Fiber 0.1g
Protein 5.9g
Total Sugars 2.3g

Chocolate & Almond Chaffle

Preparation Time: 5 minutes
Cooking Time: 12 minutes
Servings: 3

Ingredients:

- 1 egg
- ¼ cup mozzarella cheese, shredded
- 1 oz. cream cheese
- 2 teaspoons sweetener
- 1 teaspoon vanilla
- 2 tablespoons cocoa powder
- 1 teaspoon baking powder
- 2 tablespoons almonds, chopped
- 4 tablespoons almond flour

Method:

1. Blend all the ingredients in a bowl while the waffle maker is preheating.
2. Pour some of the mixture into the waffle maker.
3. Close and cook for 4 minutes.
4. Transfer the chaffle to a plate. Let cool for 2 minutes.
5. Repeat steps using the remaining mixture.

Nutritional Value:

- Calories 167
- Total Fat 13.1g
- Saturated Fat 5g
- Cholesterol 99mg
- Sodium 99mg
- Potassium 481mg
- Total Carbohydrate 9.1g
- Dietary Fiber 3.8g
- Protein 7.8g
- Total Sugars 0.8g

Bruschetta Chaffle

Preparation Time: 5 minutes
Cooking Time: 5 minutes
Servings: 2

Ingredients:

- 2 basic chaffles
- 2 tablespoons sugar-free marinara sauce
- 2 tablespoons mozzarella, shredded
- 1 tablespoon olives, sliced
- 1 tomato sliced
- 1 tablespoon keto friendly pesto sauce
- Basil leaves

Directions:

1. Spread marinara sauce on each chaffle.
2. Spoon pesto and spread on top of the marinara sauce.
3. Top with the tomato, olives and mozzarella.
4. Bake in the oven for 3 minutes or until the cheese has melted.
5. Garnish with basil.
6. Serve and enjoy.

Nutrition:

Calories 182
Total Fat 11g
Saturated Fat 6.1g
Cholesterol 30mg
Sodium 508mg
Potassium 1mg
Total Carbohydrate 3.1g
Dietary Fiber 1.1g
Protein 16.8g
Total Sugars 1g

Asian Cauliflower Chaffles

Preparation Time: 20 minutes
Cooking Time: 28 minutes
Servings: 4

Ingredients:

For the chaffles:

- 1 cup cauliflower rice, steamed
- 1 large egg, beaten
- Salt and freshly ground black pepper to taste
- 1 cup finely grated Parmesan cheese
- 1 tsp sesame seeds
- ¼ cup chopped fresh scallions

For the dipping sauce:

- 3 tbsp coconut aminos
- 1 ½ tbsp plain vinegar
- 1 tsp fresh ginger puree
- 1 tsp fresh garlic paste
- 3 tbsp sesame oil
- 1 tsp fish sauce
- 1 tsp red chili flakes

Directions:

1. Preheat the waffle iron.
2. In a medium bowl, mix the cauliflower rice, egg, salt, black pepper, and Parmesan cheese.
3. Open the iron and add a quarter of the mixture. Close and cook until crispy, 7 minutes.
4. Transfer the chaffle to a plate and make 3 more chaffles in the same manner.
5. Meanwhile, make the dipping sauce.
6. In a medium bowl, mix all the ingredients for the dipping sauce.
7. Plate the chaffles, garnish with the sesame seeds and scallions and serve with the dipping sauce.

Nutrition:
Calories 231
Fats 18.88g
Carbs 6.32g
Net Carbs 5.42g
Protein 9.66g

Hot Dog Chaffles

Preparation Time: 15 minutes
Cooking Time: 14 minutes
Servings: 2

Ingredients:

- 1 egg, beaten
- 1 cup finely grated cheddar cheese
- 2 hot dog sausages, cooked
- Mustard dressing for topping
- 8 pickle slices

Directions:

1. Preheat the waffle iron.
2. In a medium bowl, mix the egg and cheddar cheese.
3. Open the iron and add half of the mixture. Close and cook until crispy, 7 minutes.
4. Transfer the chaffle to a plate and make a second chaffle in the same manner.
5. To serve, top each chaffle with a sausage, swirl the mustard dressing on top, and then divide the pickle slices on top.
6. Enjoy!

Nutrition:

Calories 231
Fats 18.29g
Carbs 2.8g

Net Carbs 2.6g
Protein 13.39g

Spicy Shrimp and Chaffles

Preparation Time: 15 minutes
Cooking Time: 31 minutes
Servings: 4

Ingredients:

For the shrimp:

- 1 tbsp olive oil
- 1 lb jumbo shrimp, peeled and deveined
- 1 tbsp Creole seasoning
- Salt to taste

- 2 tbsp hot sauce
- 3 tbsp butter
- 2 tbsp chopped fresh scallions to garnish

For the chaffles:

- 2 eggs, beaten
- 1 cup finely grated Monterey Jack cheese

<u>Directions:</u>

For the shrimp:

1. Heat the olive oil in a medium skillet over medium heat.
2. Season the shrimp with the Creole seasoning and salt. Cook in the oil until pink and opaque on both sides, 2 minutes.
3. Pour in the hot sauce and butter. Mix well until the shrimp is adequately coated in the sauce, 1 minute.
4. Turn the heat off and set aside.

For the chaffles:

1. Preheat the waffle iron.
2. In a medium bowl, mix the eggs and Monterey Jack cheese.
3. Open the iron and add a quarter of the mixture. Close and cook until crispy, 7 minutes.
4. Transfer the chaffle to a plate and make 3 more chaffles in the same manner.
5. Cut the chaffles into quarters and place on a plate.
6. Top with the shrimp and garnish with the scallions.
7. Serve warm.

<u>**Nutrition:**</u>
Calories 342
Fats 19.75g
Carbs 2.8g
Net Carbs 2.3g
Protein 36.01g

Chicken Jalapeño Chaffles

Preparation Time: 15 minutes
Cooking Time: 14 minutes
Servings: 2

Ingredients:

- 1/8 cup finely grated Parmesan cheese
- ¼ cup finely grated cheddar cheese
- 1 egg, beaten
- ½ cup cooked chicken breasts, diced
- 1 small jalapeño pepper, deseeded and minced
- 1/8 tsp garlic powder
- 1/8 tsp onion powder
- 1 tsp cream cheese, softened

Directions:

1. Preheat the waffle iron.
2. In a medium bowl, mix all the ingredients until adequately combined.
3. Open the iron and add half of the mixture. Close and cook until crispy, 7 minutes.
4. Transfer the chaffle to a plate and make a second chaffle in the same manner.
5. Allow cooling and serve afterward.

Nutrition:
Calories 201
Fats 11.49g
Carbs 3.76g
Net Carbs 3.36g
Protein 20.11g

Chicken and Chaffle Nachos

Preparation Time: 15 minutes
Cooking Time: 33 minutes
Servings: 4

Ingredients:

For the chaffles:

- 2 eggs, beaten
- 1 cup finely grated Mexican cheese blend

For the chicken-cheese topping:

- 2 tbsp butter
- 1 tbsp almond flour
- ¼ cup unsweetened almond milk
- 1 cup finely grated cheddar cheese + more to garnish
- 3 bacon slices, cooked and chopped
- 2 cups cooked and diced chicken breasts
- 2 tbsp hot sauce
- 2 tbsp chopped fresh scallions

Directions:

For the chaffles:

1. Preheat the waffle iron.
2. In a medium bowl, mix the eggs and Mexican cheese blend.
3. Open the iron and add a quarter of the mixture. Close and cook until crispy, 7 minutes.
4. Transfer the chaffle to a plate and make 3 more chaffles in the same manner.
5. Place the chaffles on serving plates and set aside for serving.

For the chicken-cheese topping:

1. Melt the butter in a large skillet and mix in the almond flour until brown, 1 minute.
2. Pour the almond milk and whisk until well combined. Simmer until thickened, 2 minutes.

3. Stir in the cheese to melt, 2 minutes and then mix in the bacon, chicken, and hot sauce.
4. Spoon the mixture onto the chaffles and top with some more cheddar cheese.
5. Garnish with the scallions and serve immediately.

Nutrition:
Calories 524
Fats 37.51g
Carbs 3.55g
Net Carbs 3.25g
Protein 41.86g

Buffalo Hummus Beef Chaffles

Preparation Time: 15 minutes
Cooking Time: 32 minutes
Servings: 4

Ingredients:

- 2 eggs
- 1 cup + ¼ cup finely grated cheddar cheese, divided
- 2 chopped fresh scallions
- Salt and freshly ground black pepper to taste
- 2 chicken breasts, cooked and diced
- ¼ cup buffalo sauce
- 3 tbsp low-carb hummus
- 2 celery stalks, chopped
- ¼ cup crumbled blue cheese for topping

Directions:

1. Preheat the waffle iron.
2. In a medium bowl, mix the eggs, 1 cup of the cheddar cheese, scallions, salt, and black pepper,
3. Open the iron and add a quarter of the mixture. Close and cook until crispy, 7 minutes.
4. Transfer the chaffle to a plate and make 3 more chaffles in the same manner.
5. Preheat the oven to 400 F and line a baking sheet with parchment paper. Set aside.
6. Cut the chaffles into quarters and arrange on the baking sheet.
7. In a medium bowl, mix the chicken with the buffalo sauce, hummus, and celery.
8. Spoon the chicken mixture onto each quarter of chaffles and top with the remaining cheddar cheese.
9. Place the baking sheet in the oven and bake until the cheese melts, 4 minutes.
10. Remove from the oven and top with the blue cheese.
11. Serve afterward.

<u>Nutrition:</u>
Calories 552
Fats 28.37g
Carbs 6.97g
Net Carbs 6.07g
Protein 59.8g

Pulled Pork Chaffle Sandwiches

Preparation Time: 20 minutes
Cooking Time: 28 minutes
Servings: 4

Ingredients:

- 2 eggs, beaten
- 1 cup finely grated cheddar cheese
- ¼ tsp baking powder
- 2 cups cooked and shredded pork
- 1 tbsp sugar-free BBQ sauce
- 2 cups shredded coleslaw mix
- 2 tbsp apple cider vinegar
- ½ tsp salt
- ¼ cup ranch dressing

Directions:

1. Preheat the waffle iron.
2. In a medium bowl, mix the eggs, cheddar cheese, and baking powder.
3. Open the iron and add a quarter of the mixture. Close and cook until crispy, 7 minutes.
4. Transfer the chaffle to a plate and make 3 more chaffles in the same manner.
5. Meanwhile, in another medium bowl, mix the pulled pork with the BBQ sauce until well combined. Set aside.
6. Also, mix the coleslaw mix, apple cider vinegar, salt, and ranch dressing in another medium bowl.
7. When the chaffles are ready, on two pieces, divide the pork and then top with the ranch coleslaw. Cover with the remaining chaffles and insert mini skewers to secure the sandwiches.
8. Enjoy afterward.

Nutrition:

Calories 374
Fats 23.61g
Carbs 8.2g
Net Carbs 8.2g
Protein 28.05g

Okonomiyaki Chaffles

Preparation Time: 20 minutes
Cooking Time: 28 minutes
Servings: 4

Ingredients:

For the chaffles:

- 2 eggs, beaten
- 1 cup finely grated mozzarella cheese
- ½ tsp baking powder
- ¼ cup shredded radishes

For the sauce:

- 2 tsp coconut aminos
- 2 tbsp sugar-free ketchup
- 1 tbsp sugar-free maple syrup
- 2 tsp Worcestershire sauce

For the topping:

- 1 tbsp mayonnaise
- 2 tbsp chopped fresh scallions
- 2 tbsp bonito flakes
- 1 tsp dried seaweed powder
- 1 tbsp pickled ginger

Directions:

For the chaffles:

1. Preheat the waffle iron.
2. In a medium bowl, mix the eggs, mozzarella cheese, baking powder, and radishes.
3. Open the iron and add a quarter of the mixture. Close and cook until crispy, 7 minutes.
4. Transfer the chaffle to a plate and make a 3 more chaffles in the same manner.
5. For the sauce:

6. Combine the coconut aminos, ketchup, maple syrup, and Worcestershire sauce in a medium bowl and mix well.

For the topping:

1. In another mixing bowl, mix the mayonnaise, scallions, bonito flakes, seaweed powder, and ginger
2. To Servings:
3. Arrange the chaffles on four different plates and swirl the sauce on top. Spread the topping on the chaffles and serve afterward.

Nutrition:

Calories 90
Fats 3.32g
Carbs 2.97g
Net Carbs 2.17g
Protein 12.09g

Keto Reuben Chaffles

Preparation Time: 15 minutes
Cooking Time: 28 minutes
Servings: 4

Ingredients:

For the chaffles:

- 2 eggs, beaten
- 1 cup finely grated Swiss cheese
- 2 tsp caraway seeds
- 1/8 tsp salt
- ½ tsp baking powder

For the sauce:

- 2 tbsp sugar-free ketchup
- 3 tbsp mayonnaise
- 1 tbsp dill relish
- 1 tsp hot sauce

For the filling:

- 6 oz pastrami
- 2 Swiss cheese slices
- ¼ cup pickled radishes

Directions:

For the chaffles:

1. Preheat the waffle iron.
2. In a medium bowl, mix the eggs, Swiss cheese, caraway seeds, salt, and baking powder.
3. Open the iron and add a quarter of the mixture. Close and cook until crispy, 7 minutes.
4. Transfer the chaffle to a plate and make 3 more chaffles in the same manner.

For the sauce:

1. In another bowl, mix the ketchup, mayonnaise, dill relish, and hot sauce.
2. To assemble:
3. Divide on two chaffles; the sauce, the pastrami, Swiss cheese slices, and pickled radishes.
4. Cover with the other chaffles, divide the sandwich in halves and serve.

Nutrition:
Calories 316
Fats 21.78g
Carbs 6.52g
Net Carbs 5.42g
Protein 23.56g

Pumpkin-Cinnamon Churro Sticks

Preparation Time: 10 minutes
Cooking Time: 14 minutes
Servings: 2

Ingredients:

- 3 tbsp coconut flour
- ¼ cup pumpkin puree
- 1 egg, beaten
- ½ cup finely grated mozzarella cheese
- 2 tbsp sugar-free maple syrup + more for serving
- 1 tsp baking powder
- 1 tsp vanilla extract
- ½ tsp pumpkin spice seasoning
- 1/8 tsp salt
- 1 tbsp cinnamon powder

Directions:

1. Preheat the waffle iron.
2. Mix all the ingredients in a medium bowl until well combined.
3. Open the iron and add half of the mixture. Close and cook until golden brown and crispy, 7 minutes.
4. Remove the chaffle onto a plate and make 1 more with the remaining batter.
5. Cut each chaffle into sticks, drizzle the top with more maple syrup and serve after.

Nutrition Facts per Serving:
Calories 219
Fats 9.72g
Carbs 8.64g
Net Carbs 4.34g
Protein 25.27g

Keto Chocolate Fudge Chaffle

Preparation Time: 10 minutes
Cooking Time: 14 minutes
Servings: 2

Ingredients:

- 1 egg, beaten
- ¼ cup finely grated Gruyere cheese
- 2 tbsp unsweetened cocoa powder
- ¼ tsp baking powder
- ¼ tsp vanilla extract
- 2 tbsp erythritol
- 1 tsp almond flour
- 1 tsp heavy whipping cream
- A pinch of salt

Directions:

1. Preheat the waffle iron.
2. Add all the ingredients to a medium bowl and mix well.
3. Open the iron and add half of the mixture. Close and cook until golden brown and crispy, 7 minutes.
4. Remove the chaffle onto a plate and make another with the remaining batter.
5. Cut each chaffle into wedges and serve after.

Nutrition Facts per Serving:

Calories 173
Fats 13.08g
Carbs 3.98g
Net Carbs 2.28g
Protein 12.27g

Guacamole Chaffle Bites

Preparation Time: 10 minutes
Cooking Time: 14 minutes
Servings: 2

Ingredients:

- 1 large turnip, cooked and mashed
- 2 bacon slices, cooked and finely chopped
- ½ cup finely grated Monterey Jack cheese
- 1 egg, beaten
- 1 cup guacamole for topping

Directions:

1. Preheat the waffle iron.
2. Mix all the ingredients except for the guacamole in a medium bowl.
3. Open the iron and add half of the mixture. Close and cook for 4 minutes. Open the lid, flip the chaffle and cook further until golden brown and crispy, 3 minutes.
4. Remove the chaffle onto a plate and make another in the same manner.
5. Cut each chaffle into wedges, top with the guacamole and serve afterward.

Nutrition Facts per Serving:

Calories 311
Fats 22.52g
Carbs 8.29g
Net Carbs 5.79g
Protein 13.62g

Zucchini Parmesan Chaffles

Preparation Time: 10 minutes
Cooking Time: 14 minutes
Servings: 2

Ingredients:

- 1 cup shredded zucchini
- 1 egg, beaten
- ½ cup finely grated Parmesan cheese
- Salt and freshly ground black pepper to taste

Directions:

1. Preheat the waffle iron.
2. Put all the ingredients in a medium bowl and mix well.
3. Open the iron and add half of the mixture. Close and cook until crispy, 7 minutes.
4. Remove the chaffle onto a plate and make another with the remaining mixture.
5. Cut each chaffle into wedges and serve afterward.

Nutrition Facts per Serving:

Calories 138
Fats 9.07g
Carbs 3.81g
Net Carbs 3.71g
Protein 10.02g

40. Blue Cheese Chaffle Bites

Preparation Time: 10 minutes
Cooking Time: 14 minutes
Servings: 2

Ingredients:

- 1 egg, beaten
- ½ cup finely grated Parmesan cheese
- ¼ cup crumbled blue cheese
- 1 tsp erythritol

Directions:

1. Preheat the waffle iron.
2. Mix all the ingredients in a bowl.
3. Open the iron and add half of the mixture. Close and cook until crispy, 7 minutes.
4. Remove the chaffle onto a plate and make another with the remaining mixture.
5. Cut each chaffle into wedges and serve afterward.

Nutrition Facts per Serving:

Calories 196
Fats 13.91g
Carbs 4.03g
Net Carbs 4.03g
Protein 13.48g

Intermediate

Pumpkin Chaffle with Frosting

Preparation Time: 15 minutes
Servings: 2

Ingredients:

- 1 egg, lightly beaten
- 1 tbsp sugar-free pumpkin puree
- 1/4 tsp pumpkin pie spice
- 1/2 cup mozzarella cheese, shredded

For frosting:

- 1/2 tsp vanilla
- 2 tbsp Swerve
- 2 tbsp cream cheese, softened

Directions:

1. Preheat your waffle maker.
2. Add egg in a bowl and whisk well.
3. Add pumpkin puree, pumpkin pie spice, and cheese and stir well.
4. Spray waffle maker with cooking spray.
5. Pour 1/2 of the batter in the hot waffle maker and cook for 3-4 minutes or until golden brown. Repeat with the remaining batter.
6. In a small bowl, mix all frosting ingredients until smooth.
7. Add frosting on top of hot chaffles and serve.

Nutrition:

Calories 98
Fat 7 g
Carbohydrates 3.6 g
Sugar 0.6 g
Protein 5.6 g
Cholesterol 97 mg

Breakfast Peanut Butter Chaffle

Preparation Time: 15 minutes

Servings: 2

Ingredients:

- 1 egg, lightly beaten
- ½ tsp vanilla
- 1 tbsp Swerve
- 2 tbsp powdered peanut butter
- ½ cup mozzarella cheese, shredded

Directions:

1. Preheat your waffle maker.
2. Add all ingredients into the bowl and mix until well combined.
3. Spray waffle maker with cooking spray.
4. Pour half batter in the hot waffle maker and cook for 5-7 minutes or until golden brown. Repeat with the remaining batter.
5. Serve and enjoy.

Nutrition:

Calories 80

Fat 4.1 g

Carbohydrates 2.9 g

Sugar 0.6 g

Protein 7.4 g

Cholesterol 86 mg

Chaffles with Caramelized Apples and Yogurt

Serving: 2
Preparation Time: 5 minutes
Cooking Time: 10 minutes

Ingredients

- 1 tablespoon unsalted butter
- 1 tablespoon golden brown sugar
- 1 Granny Smith apple, cored and thinly sliced
- 1 pinch salt
- 2 whole-grain frozen waffles, toasted
- 1/2 cup mozzarella cheese, shredded
- 1/4 cup Yoplait® Original French Vanilla yogurt

Direction

1. Melt the butter in a large skillet over medium-high heat until starting to brown. Add mozzarella cheese and stir well.
2. Add the sugar, apple slices and salt and cook, stirring frequently, until apples are softened and tender, about 6 to 9 minutes.
3. Put one warm waffle each on a plate, top each with yogurt and apples. Serve warm.

Nutrition:

Calories: 240 calories
Total Fat: 10.4 g
Cholesterol: 54 mg
Sodium: 226 mg
Total Carbohydrate: 33.8 g
Protein: 4.7 g

Chaffle Ice Cream Bowl

Preparation Time: 5 minutes

Cooking Time: 0 minutes

Servings: 2

Ingredients:
- 4 basic chaffles
- 2 scoops keto ice cream
- 2 teaspoons sugar-free chocolate syrup

Method:
1. Arrange 2 basic chaffles in a bowl, following the contoured design of the bowl.
2. Top with the ice cream.
3. Drizzle with the syrup on top.
4. Serve.

Nutritional Value:
- Calories 181
- Total Fat 17.2g
- Saturated Fat 4.2g
- Cholesterol 26mg
- Sodium 38mg
- Total Carbohydrate 7g
- Dietary Fiber 1g
- Total Sugars 4.1g
- Protein 0.4g
- Potassium 0mg

70. Zucchini Chaffle

Preparation Time: 10 minutes

Cooking Time: 8 minutes

Servings: 2

Ingredients:

- 1 cup zucchini, grated
- ¼ cup mozzarella cheese, shredded
- 1 egg, beaten
- ½ cup Parmesan cheese, shredded
- 1 teaspoon dried basil
- Salt and pepper to taste

Method:

1. Preheat your waffle maker.
2. Sprinkle pinch of salt over the zucchini and mix.
3. Let sit for 2 minutes.
4. Wrap zucchini with paper towel and squeeze to get rid of water.
5. Transfer to a bowl and stir in the rest of the ingredients.
6. Pour half of the mixture into the waffle maker.
7. Close the device.
8. Cook for 4 minutes.
9. Make the second chaffle following the same steps.

Nutritional Value:

- Calories 194
- Total Fat 13 g
- Saturated Fat 7 g
- Cholesterol 115 mg
- Sodium 789 mg
- Potassium 223 mg
- Total Carbohydrate 4 g
- Dietary Fiber 1 g
- Protein 16 g
- Total Sugars 2 g

Chaffle Cream Cake

Preparation Time: 20 minutes

Cooking Time: 30 minutes

Servings: 8

Ingredients:

Chaffle

- 4 oz. cream cheese
- 4 eggs
- 1 tablespoon butter, melted
- 1 teaspoon vanilla extract
- ½ teaspoon cinnamon
- 1 tablespoon sweetener
- 4 tablespoons coconut flour
- 1 tablespoon almond flour
- 1 ½ teaspoons baking powder
- 1 tablespoon coconut flakes (sugar-free)
- 1 tablespoon walnuts, chopped

Frosting

- 2 oz. cream cheese
- 2 tablespoons butter
- 2 tablespoons sweetener
- ½ teaspoon vanilla

Method:

1. Combine all the chaffle ingredients except coconut flakes and walnuts in a blender.
2. Blend until smooth.
3. Plug in your waffle maker.
4. Add some of the mixture to the waffle maker.
5. Cook for 3 minutes.
6. Repeat steps until the remaining batter is used.
7. While letting the chaffles cool, make the frosting by combining all the ingredients.

250

8. Use a mixer to combine and turn frosting into fluffy consistency.
9. Spread the frosting on top of the chaffles.

Nutritional Value:
- Calories127
- Total Fat 13.7g
- Saturated Fat 9 g
- Cholesterol 102.9mg
- Sodium 107.3mg
- Potassium 457 mg
- Total Carbohydrate 5.5g
- Dietary Fiber 1.3g
- Protein 5.3g
- Total Sugars 1.5g

Taco Chaffle

>Preparation Time: 15 minutes
>
>Cooking Time: 20 minutes
>
>Servings: 4

Ingredients:

- 1 tablespoon olive oil
- 1 lb. ground beef
- 1 teaspoon ground cumin
- 1 teaspoon chili powder
- ¼ teaspoon onion powder
- ½ teaspoon garlic powder
- Salt to taste
- 4 basic chaffles
- 1 cup cabbage, chopped
- 4 tablespoons salsa (sugar-free)

Method:

1. Pour the olive oil into a pan over medium heat.
2. Add the ground beef.
3. Season with the salt and spices.
4. Cook until brown and crumbly.
5. Fold the chaffle to create a "taco shell".
6. Stuff each chaffle taco with cabbage.
7. Top with the ground beef and salsa.

Nutritional Value:

- Calories 255
- Total Fat 10.9g
- Saturated Fat 3.2g
- Cholesterol 101mg
- Sodium 220mg
- Potassium 561mg
- Total Carbohydrate 3g
- Dietary Fiber 1g
- Protein 35.1g
- Total Sugars 1.3g

Chicken Parmesan Chaffle

Preparation Time: 15 minutes

Cooking Time: 8 minutes

Servings: 2

Ingredients:

Chaffle

- 1 egg, beaten
- ¼ cup cheddar cheese, shredded
- 1/8 cup Parmesan cheese, grated
- 1 teaspoon cream cheese
- ½ cup chicken breast meat, shredded
- 1/8 teaspoon garlic powder
- 1 teaspoon Italian seasoning

Toppings

- 1 tablespoon pizza sauce (sugar-free)
- 2 provolone cheese slices

Method:

1. Plug in your waffle maker.
2. Combine all the chaffle ingredients in a bowl.
3. Mix well.
4. Add half of the mixture to the waffle maker.
5. Cook for 4 minutes.
6. Repeat with the next chaffle.
7. Spread the pizza sauce on top of each chaffle and put Provolone on top.

Nutritional Value:

- Calories125
- Total Fat 8.3g
- Saturated Fat 4 g
- Cholesterol 115.3mg
- Sodium 285.7mg
- Potassium 760 mg
- Total Carbohydrate 2.6g
- Dietary Fiber 0.3g
- Protein 9.4g

Cheese Garlic Chaffle

Preparation Time: 10 minutes

Cooking Time: 8 minutes

Servings: 2

<u>Ingredients:</u>

Chaffle

- 1 egg
- 1 teaspoon cream cheese
- ½ cup mozzarella cheese, shredded
- ½ teaspoon garlic powder
- 1 teaspoon Italian seasoning

Topping

- 1 tablespoon butter
- ½ teaspoon garlic powder
- ½ teaspoon Italian seasoning
- 2 tablespoon mozzarella cheese, shredded

<u>Method:</u>

1. Plug in your waffle maker to preheat.
2. Preheat your oven to 350 degrees F.
3. In a bowl, combine all the chaffle ingredients.
4. Cook in the waffle maker for 4 minutes per chaffle.
5. Transfer to a baking pan.
6. Spread butter on top of each chaffle.
7. Sprinkle garlic powder and Italian seasoning on top.
8. Top with mozzarella cheese.
9. Bake until the cheese has melted.

Nutritional Value:

- Calories 141
- Total Fat 13 g
- Saturated Fat 8 g
- Cholesterol 115.8 mg
- Sodium 255.8 mg
- Potassium 350 mg
- Total Carbohydrate 2.6g
- Dietary Fiber 0.7g

Chicken Chaffle Sandwich

Preparation Time: 5 minutes

Cooking Time: 15 minutes

Servings: 2

Ingredients:
- 1 chicken breast fillet, sliced into strips
- Salt and pepper to taste
- 1 teaspoon dried rosemary
- 1 tablespoon olive oil
- 4 basic chaffles
- 2 tablespoons butter, melted
- 2 tablespoons Parmesan cheese, grated

Method:
1. Season the chicken strips with salt, pepper and rosemary.
2. Add olive oil to a pan over medium low heat.
3. Cook the chicken until brown on both sides.
4. Spread butter on top of each chaffle.
5. Sprinkle cheese on top.
6. Place the chicken on top and top with another chaffle.

Nutritional Value:
- Calories 262
- Total Fat 20g
- Saturated Fat 9.2g
- Cholesterol 77mg
- Sodium 270mg
- Potassium 125mg
- Total Carbohydrate 1g
- Dietary Fiber 0.2g
- Protein 20.2g
- Total Sugars 0g

Cornbread Chaffle

Preparation Time: 5 minutes

Cooking Time: 8 minutes

Servings: 2

Ingredients:

- 1 egg, beaten
- ½ cup cheddar cheese, shredded
- 5 slices pickled jalapeno, chopped and drained
- 1 teaspoon hot sauce
- ¼ teaspoon corn extract
- Salt to taste

Method:

1. Combine all the ingredients in a bowl while preheating your waffle maker.
2. Add half of the mixture to the device.
3. Seal and cook for 4 minutes.
4. Let cool on a plate for 2 minutes.
5. Repeat steps for the second chaffle.

Nutritional Value:

- Calories150
- Total Fat 11.8g
- Saturated Fat 7 g
- Cholesterol 121mg
- Sodium 1399.4mg
- Potassium 350 mg
- Total Carbohydrate 1.1g
- Dietary Fiber 0g
- Protein 9.6g
- Total Sugars 0.2g

Italian Sausage Chaffles

Preparation Time: 5 minutes

Cooking Time: 8 minutes

Servings: 2

Ingredients:

- 1 egg, beaten
- 1 cup cheddar cheese, shredded
- ¼ cup Parmesan cheese, grated
- 1 lb. Italian sausage, crumbled
- 2 teaspoons baking powder
- 1 cup almond flour

Method:

1. Preheat your waffle maker.
2. Mix all the ingredients in a bowl.
3. Pour half of the mixture into the waffle maker.
4. Cover and cook for 4 minutes.
5. Transfer to a plate.
6. Let cool to make it crispy.
7. Do the same steps to make the next chaffle.

Nutritional Value:

- Calories 332
- Total Fat 27.1g
- Saturated Fat 10.2g
- Cholesterol 98mg
- Sodium 634mg
- Total Carbohydrate 1.9g
- Dietary Fiber 0.5g
- Total Sugars 0.1g
- Protein 19.6g
- Potassium 359mg

LT Chaffle Sandwich

Preparation Time: 10 minutes

Cooking Time: 15 minutes

Servings: 2

<u>Ingredients:</u>

- Cooking spray
- 4 slices bacon
- 1 tablespoon mayonnaise
- 4 basic chaffles
- 2 lettuce leaves
- 2 tomato slices

<u>Method:</u>

1. Coat your pan with foil and place it over medium heat.
2. Cook the bacon until golden and crispy.
3. Spread mayo on top of the chaffle.
4. Top with the lettuce, bacon and tomato.
5. Top with another chaffle.

<u>Nutritional Value:</u>

- Calories 238
- Total Fat 18.4g
- Saturated Fat 5.6g
- Cholesterol 44mg
- Sodium 931mg
- Potassium 258mg
- Total Carbohydrate 3g
- Dietary Fiber 0.2g
- Protein 14.3g
- Total Sugars 0.9g

Sloppy Joe Chaffle

Preparation Time: 15 minutes

Cooking Time: 15 minutes

Servings: 2

Ingredients:

- 1 teaspoon olive oil
- 1 lb. ground beef
- Salt and pepper to taste
- 1 teaspoon onion powder
- 1 teaspoon garlic powder
- 3 tablespoons tomato paste
- 1 tablespoon chili powder
- 1 teaspoon mustard powder
- ½ teaspoon paprika
- ½ cup beef broth
- 1 teaspoon coconut aminos
- 1 teaspoon sweetener
- 4 cornbread chaffles

Method:

1. Pour the olive oil into a pan over medium high heat.
2. Add the ground beef.
3. Season with salt, pepper and spices.
4. Cook for 5 minutes, stirring occasionally.
5. Stir in the beef broth, coconut aminos and sweetener.
6. Reduce heat and simmer for 10 minutes.
7. Top the cornbread chaffle with the ground beef mixture.
8. Top with another chaffle.

Nutritional Value:

- Calories 334
- Total Fat 12.1g
- Saturated Fat 4g
- Cholesterol 135mg
- Sodium 269mg
- Potassium 887mg
- Total Carbohydrate 6.5g
- Dietary Fiber 2g
- Protein 48.2g
- Total Sugars 2.9g

Peanut Butter Chaffle Cake

Preparation Time: 10 minutes

Cooking Time: 10 minutes

Servings: 2

Ingredients:

Chaffle

- 1 egg, beaten
- ¼ teaspoon baking powder
- 2 tablespoons peanut butter powder (sugar-free)
- ¼ teaspoon peanut butter extract
- 1 tablespoon heavy whipping cream
- 2 tablespoons sweetener

Frosting

- 2 tablespoons sweetener
- 1 tablespoon butter
- 1 tablespoon peanut butter (sugar-free)
- 2 tablespoons cream cheese
- ¼ teaspoon vanilla

Method:

1. Preheat your waffle maker.
2. In a large bowl, combine all the ingredients for the chaffle.
3. Pour half of the mixture into the waffle maker.
4. Seal and cook for 4 minutes.
5. Repeat steps to make the second chaffle.
6. While letting the chaffles cool, add the frosting ingredients in a bowl.
7. Use a mixer to turn mixture into fluffy frosting.
8. Spread the frosting on top of the chaffles and serve.

Nutritional Value:

- Calories192
- Total Fat 17 g
- Saturated Fat 8 g
- Cholesterol 97.1 mg
- Sodium 64.3 mg
- Potassium 342 mg
- Total Carbohydrate 3.6 g
- Dietary Fiber 0.6 g
- Protein 5.5 g
- Total Sugars 1.8 g

Garlic Cauliflower Chaffle

Preparation Time: 5 minutes

Cooking Time: 8 minutes

Servings: 2

Ingredients:

- 1 egg, beaten
- 1 cup cauliflower rice
- ½ cup cheddar cheese, shredded
- 1 teaspoon garlic powder

Method:

1. Plug in your waffle maker.
2. Mix all the ingredients in a bowl.
3. Transfer half of the mixture to the waffle maker.
4. Close the device and cook for 4 minutes.
5. Put the chaffle on a plate to cool for 2 minutes.
6. Repeat procedure to make the next chaffle.

Nutritional Value:

- Calories 178
- Total Fat 12.5g
- Saturated Fat 7g
- Cholesterol 112mg
- Sodium 267mg
- Total Carbohydrate 4.9g
- Dietary Fiber 0.1g
- Total Sugars 2.7g
- Protein 12g
- Potassium 73mg

•

82. Apple Pie Chaffle

Preparation Time: 5 minutes

Cooking Time: 8 minutes

Servings: 2

Ingredients:

- 1 egg
- ½ cup mozzarella cheese
- 1 teaspoon apple pie spice
- 1 tablespoon chocolate chips (sugar-free)

Method:

1. Mix all the ingredients in a bowl while the waffle maker is preheating.
2. Add half of the mixture into the waffle maker.
3. Seal. Cook for 4 minutes.
4. Put the chaffle on a plate to cool for 2 minutes.
5. Repeat the steps to cook the second chaffle.

Nutritional Value:

- Calories 165
- Total Fat 10.2g
- Saturated Fat 5.2g
- Cholesterol 174mg
- Sodium 156mg
- Total Carbohydrate 8.3g
- Dietary Fiber 0.6g
- Total Sugars 5.9g
- Protein 10.4g
- Potassium 109mg

83. Basic Chaffle

Preparation Time: 5 minutes
Cooking Time: 8 minutes
Serving: 2

Ingredients:

- Cooking spray
- 1 egg
- ½ cup cheddar cheese, shredded

Method:

1. Turn your waffle maker on.
2. Grease both sides with cooking spray.
3. Beat the egg in a bowl.
4. Stir in the cheddar cheese.
5. Pour half of the batter into the waffle maker.
6. Seal and cook for 4 minutes.
7. Remove the chaffle slowly from the waffle maker.
8. Let sit for 3 minutes.
9. Pour the remaining batter into the waffle maker and repeat the steps.

Nutritional Value:

- Calories 191
- Total Fat 23 g
- Saturated Fat 14 g
- Cholesterol 223 mg
- Sodium 413 mg
- Potassium 116 mg
- Total Carbohydrate 1 g
- Dietary Fiber 1 g
- Protein 20 g
- Total Sugars 1 g

Keto Chaffle with Almond Flour
Preparation Time: 5 minutes
Cooking Time: 8 minutes
Servings: 2
Ingredients:
- 1 egg, beaten
- ½ cup cheddar cheese, shredded
- 1 tablespoon almond flour

Method:
1. Turn on your waffle maker.
2. Mix all the ingredients in a bowl.
3. Pour half of the batter into the waffle maker.
4. Close the device and cook for 4 minutes.
5. Remove from the waffle maker.
6. Let sit for 2 to 3 minutes.
7. Repeat the steps with the remaining batter.

Nutritional Value:
- Calories 145
- Total Fat 11 g
- Saturated Fat 7 g
- Cholesterol 112 mg
- Sodium 207 mg
- Potassium 158 mg
- Total Carbohydrate 1 g
- Dietary Fiber 1 g
- Protein 10 g
- Total Sugars 1 g

Garlic Chaffle
Preparation Time: 5 minutes

Cooking Time: 8 minutes

Serving: 2

Ingredients:
- 1 egg
- ½ cup cheddar cheese, beaten

- 1 teaspoon coconut flour
- Pinch garlic powder

Method:

1. Plug in your waffle maker.
2. Beat the egg in a bowl.
3. Stir in the rest of the ingredients.
4. Pour half of the batter into your waffle maker.
5. Cook for 4 minutes.
6. Remove the waffle and let sit for 2 minutes.
7. Do the same steps with the remaining batter.

Nutritional Value:
- Calories 170
- Total Fat 14 g
- Saturated Fat 6 g
- Cholesterol 121 mg
- Sodium 220 mg
- Potassium 165 mg
- Total Carbohydrate 2 g
- Dietary Fiber 1 g
- Protein 10 g
- Total Sugars 1 g

Bacon Chaffle

Preparation Time: 5 minutes

Cooking Time: 8 minutes

Servings: 2

Ingredients:

- 1 egg
- ½ cup cheddar cheese, shredded
- 1 teaspoon baking powder
- 2 tablespoons almond flour
- 3 tablespoons bacon bits, cooked

Method:

1. Turn your waffle maker on.
2. Beat the egg in a bowl.
3. Stir in the cheese, baking powder, almond flour and bacon bits.
4. Pour half of the batter into the waffle maker.
5. Close the device.
6. Cook for 4 minutes.
7. Open and transfer waffle on a plate. Let cool for 2 minutes.
8. Repeat the same procedure with the remaining batter.

Nutritional Value:

- Calories 147
- Total Fat 11.5 g
- Saturated Fat 5.4 g
- Cholesterol 88 mg
- Sodium 286 mg
- Potassium 243 mg
- Total Carbohydrate 1.7 g
- Dietary Fiber 1 g
- Protein 9.8 g
- Total Sugars 1 g

Blueberry Chaffle

Preparation Time: 10 minutes

Cooking Time: 8 minutes

Servings: 2

Ingredients:

- 1 egg, beaten
- ½ cup mozzarella cheese, shredded
- 1 teaspoon baking powder
- 2 tablespoons almond flour
- 2 teaspoons sweetener
- ¼ cup blueberries, chopped

Method:

1. Combine all the ingredients in a bowl. Mix well.
2. Turn on the waffle maker.
3. Pour half of the mixture into the cooking device.
4. Close it and cook for 4 minutes.
5. Open the waffle maker and transfer to a plate.
6. Let cool for 2 minutes.
7. Add the remaining mixture to the waffle maker and repeat the steps.

Nutritional Value:

- Calories 175
- Total Fat 4.3g
- Saturated Fat 1.5g
- Cholesterol 86mg
- Sodium 76mg
- Potassium 296mg
- Total Carbohydrate 6.6g
- Dietary Fiber 1.7g
- Protein 5.3g
- Total Sugars 2g

Cinnamon Chaffle

Preparation Time: 5 minutes

Cooking Time: 8 minutes

Servings: 2

Ingredients:

- 1 egg
- ½ cup of mozzarella cheese, shredded
- 2 tablespoons almond flour
- 1 teaspoon baking powder
- 1 teaspoon vanilla
- 2 teaspoons cinnamon
- 1 teaspoon sweetener

Method:

1. Preheat your waffle maker.
2. Beat the egg in a bowl.
3. Stir in the rest of the ingredients.
4. Transfer half of the batter into the waffle maker.
5. Close and cook for 4 minutes.
6. Open and put the waffle on a plate. Let cool for 2 minutes.
7. Do the same steps for the remaining batter.

Nutritional Value:

- Calories 136
- Total Fat 7.4g
- Saturated Fat 2.9g
- Cholesterol 171mg
- Sodium 152mg
- Potassium 590mg
- Total Carbohydrate 9.6g
- Dietary Fiber 3.6g
- Protein 9.9g
- Total Sugars 1g

Nut Butter Chaffle

Preparation Time: 10 minutes

Cooking Time: 8 minutes

Servings: 2

Ingredients:

- 1 egg
- ½ cup mozzarella cheese, shredded
- 2 tablespoons almond flour
- ½ teaspoon baking powder
- 1 tablespoon sweetener
- 1 teaspoon vanilla
- 2 tablespoons nut butter

Method:

1. Turn on the waffle maker.
2. Beat the egg in a bowl and combine with the cheese.
3. In another bowl, mix the almond flour, baking powder and sweetener.
4. In the third bowl, blend the vanilla extract and nut butter.
5. Gradually add the almond flour mixture into the egg mixture.
6. Then, stir in the vanilla extract.
7. Pour the batter into the waffle maker.
8. Cook for 4 minutes.
9. Transfer to a plate and let cool for 2 minutes.
10. Repeat the steps with the remaining batter.

Nutritional Value:

- Calories 168
- Total Fat 15.5g
- Saturated Fat 3.9g
- Cholesterol 34mg
- Sodium 31mg
- Potassium 64mg
- Total Carbohydrate 1.6g
- Dietary Fiber 1.4g
- Protein 5.4g
- Total Sugars 0.6g

Expert

90. Lemon Chaffle

Preparation Time: 10 minutes

Cooking Time: 12 minutes

Servings: 3-4

<u>Ingredients:</u>
- 1 egg
- ¼ cup mozzarella cheese, shredded
- 1 oz. cream cheese
- 2 teaspoons lemon juice
- 2 tablespoons sweetener
- 1 teaspoon baking powder
- 4 tablespoons almond flour

<u>Method:</u>
1. Preheat your waffle maker.
2. Beat the egg in a bowl.
3. Stir in the two cheeses.
4. Add the remaining ingredients.
5. Mix well.
6. Pour batter into the waffle maker.
7. Cook for 4 minutes.
8. Open and let waffle cook for 2 minutes.
9. Add the remaining batter to the device and repeat the steps.

Nutritional Value:

- Calories 166
- Total Fat 9.5g
- Saturated Fat 4.3g
- Cholesterol 99mg
- Sodium 99mg
- Potassium 305mg
- Total Carbohydrate 3.7g
- Dietary Fiber 1g
- Protein 5.6g

Banana Nut Muffin

Preparation Time: 10 minutes

Cooking Time: 12 minutes

Servings: 3-4

Ingredients:

- 1 egg
- 1 oz. cream cheese
- ¼ cup mozzarella cheese, shredded
- 1 teaspoon banana extract
- 2 tablespoons sweetener
- 1 teaspoon baking powder
- 4 tablespoons almond flour
- 2 tablespoons walnuts, chopped

Method:

1. Combine all the ingredients in a bowl.
2. Turn on the waffle maker.
3. Add the batter to the waffle maker.
4. Seal and cook for 4 minutes.
5. Open and transfer the waffle to a plate. Let cool for 2 minutes.
6. Do the same steps with the remaining mixture.

Nutritional Value:

- Calories 169
- Total Fat 14g
- Saturated Fat 4.6g
- Cholesterol 99mg
- Sodium 98mg
- Potassium 343mg
- Total Carbohydrate 5.6g
- Dietary Fiber 2g
- Protein 7.5g
- Total Sugars 0.6g

Pizza Flavored Chaffle

Preparation Time: 10 minutes

Cooking Time: 12 minutes

Servings: 3

Ingredients:

- 1 egg, beaten
- ½ cup cheddar cheese, shredded
- 2 tablespoons pepperoni, chopped
- 1 tablespoon keto marinara sauce
- 4 tablespoons almond flour
- 1 teaspoon baking powder
- ½ teaspoon dried Italian seasoning
- Parmesan cheese, grated

Method:

1. Preheat your waffle maker.
2. In a bowl, mix the egg, cheddar cheese, pepperoni, marinara sauce, almond flour, baking powder and Italian seasoning.
3. Add the mixture to the waffle maker.
4. Close the device and cook for 4 minutes.
5. Open it and transfer chaffle to a plate.
6. Let cool for 2 minutes.
7. Repeat the steps with the remaining batter.
8. Top with the grated Parmesan and serve.

Nutritional Value:

- Calories 179
- Total Fat 14.3g
- Saturated Fat 7.5g
- Cholesterol 118mg
- Sodium 300mg
- Potassium 326mg
- Total Carbohydrate 1.8g
- Dietary Fiber 0.1g
- Protein 11.1g
- Total Sugars 0.4g

Chocolate Chaffle

Preparation Time: 5 minutes

Cooking Time: 8 minutes

Servings: 2

Ingredients:

- 1 egg
- ½ cup mozzarella cheese, shredded
- ½ teaspoon baking powder
- 2 tablespoons cocoa powder
- 2 tablespoons sweetener
- 2 tablespoons almond flour

Method:

1. Turn your waffle maker on.
2. Beat the egg in a bowl.
3. Stir in the rest of the ingredients.
4. Put the mixture into the waffle maker.
5. Seal the device and cook for 4 minutes.
6. Open and transfer the chaffle to a plate to cool for 2 minutes.
7. Do the same steps using the remaining mixture.

Nutritional Value:

- Calories 149
- Total Fat 10.8g
- Saturated Fat 2.4g
- Cholesterol 86mg
- Sodium 80mg
- Potassium 291mg
- Total Carbohydrate 9g
- Dietary Fiber 4.1g
- Protein 8.8g
- Total Sugars 0.3g

Maple Syrup & Vanilla Chaffle
Preparation Time: 10 minutes

Cooking Time: 12 minutes

Servings: 3

Ingredients:

- 1 egg, beaten
- ¼ cup mozzarella cheese, shredded
- 1 oz. cream cheese
- 1 teaspoon vanilla
- 1 tablespoon keto maple syrup
- 1 teaspoon sweetener
- 1 teaspoon baking powder
- 4 tablespoons almond flour

Method:

1. Preheat your waffle maker.
2. Add all the ingredients to a bowl.
3. Mix well.
4. Pour some of the batter into the waffle maker.
5. Cover and cook for 4 minutes.
6. Transfer chaffle to a plate and let cool for 2 minutes.
7. Repeat the same process with the remaining mixture.

Nutritional Value:

- Calories 146
- Total Fat 9.5g
- Saturated Fat 4.3g
- Cholesterol 99mg
- Potassium 322mg
- Sodium 99mg
- Total Carbohydrate 10.6g
- Dietary Fiber 0.9g
- Protein 5.6g
- Total Sugars 6.4g

Red Velvet Chaffle

Preparation Time: 5 minutes

Cooking Time: 12 minutes

Servings: 3

<u>Ingredients:</u>

- 1 egg
- ¼ cup mozzarella cheese, shredded
- 1 oz. cream cheese
- 4 tablespoons almond flour
- 1 teaspoon baking powder
- 2 teaspoons sweetener
- 1 teaspoon red velvet extract
- 2 tablespoons cocoa powder

<u>Method:</u>

1. Combine all the ingredients in a bowl.
2. Plug in your waffle maker.
3. Pour some of the batter into the waffle maker.
4. Seal and cook for 4 minutes.
5. Open and transfer to a plate.
6. Repeat the steps with the remaining batter.

Nutritional Value:

- Calories 126
- Total Fat 10.1g
- Saturated Fat 3.4g
- Cholesterol 66mg
- Sodium 68mg
- Potassium 290mg
- Total Carbohydrate 6.5g
- Dietary Fiber 2.8g
- Protein 5.9g
- Total Sugars 0.2g

Chaffle Tortilla

Preparation Time: 5 minutes

Cooking Time: 8 minutes

Servings: 2

Ingredients:

- 1 egg
- ½ cup cheddar cheese, shredded
- 1 teaspoon baking powder
- 4 tablespoons almond flour
- ¼ teaspoon garlic powder
- 1 tablespoon almond milk
- Homemade salsa
- Sour cream
- Jalapeno pepper, chopped

Method:

1. Preheat your waffle maker.
2. Beat the egg in a bowl.
3. Stir in the cheese, baking powder, flour, garlic powder and almond milk.
4. Pour half of the batter into the waffle maker.
5. Cover and cook for 4 minutes.
6. Open and transfer to a plate. Let cool for 2 minutes.
7. Do the same for the remaining batter.
8. Top the waffle with salsa, sour cream and jalapeno pepper.
9. Roll the waffle.

Nutritional Value:
- Calories 225
- Total Fat 17.6g
- Saturated Fat 9.9g
- Cholesterol 117mg
- Sodium 367mg
- Potassium 366mg
- Total Carbohydrate 6g
- Dietary Fiber 0.8g
- Protein 11.3g
- Total Sugars 1.9g

Churro Chaffle

Preparation Time: 5 minutes

Cooking Time: 8 minutes

Servings: 2

<u>Ingredients:</u>

- 1 egg
- ½ cup mozzarella cheese, shredded
- ½ teaspoon cinnamon
- 2 tablespoons sweetener

<u>Method:</u>

1. Turn on your waffle iron.
2. Beat the egg in a bowl.
3. Stir in the cheese.
4. Pour half of the mixture into the waffle maker.
5. Cover the waffle iron.
6. Cook for 4 minutes.
7. While waiting, mix the cinnamon and sweetener in a bowl.
8. Open the device and soak the waffle in the cinnamon mixture.
9. Repeat the steps with the remaining batter.

<u>**Nutritional Value:**</u>

- Calories 106
- Total Fat 6.9g
- Saturated Fat 2.9g
- Cholesterol 171mg
- Sodium 147mg
- Potassium 64mg
- Total Carbohydrate 5.8g
- Dietary Fiber 2.6g
- Protein 9.6g
- Total Sugars 0.4g

Chocolate Chip Chaffle

Preparation Time: 5 minutes

Cooking Time: 8 minutes

Servings: 2

Ingredients:

- 1 egg
- ½ teaspoon coconut flour
- ¼ teaspoon baking powder
- 1 teaspoon sweetener
- 1 tablespoon heavy whipping cream
- 1 tablespoon chocolate chips

Method:

1. Preheat your waffle maker.
2. Beat the egg in a bowl.
3. Stir in the flour, baking powder, sweetener and cream.
4. Pour half of the mixture into the waffle maker.
5. Sprinkle the chocolate chips on top and close.
6. Cook for 4 minutes.
7. Remove the chaffle and put on a plate.
8. Do the same procedure with the remaining batter.

Nutritional Value:

- Calories 146
- Total Fat 10 g
- Saturated Fat 7 g
- Cholesterol 88 mg
- Sodium 140 mg
- Potassium 50 mg
- Total Carbohydrate 5 g
- Dietary Fiber 3 g
- Protein 6 g
- Total Sugars 1 g

Breakfast Chaffle Sandwich

Preparation Time: 10 minutes

Cooking Time: 10 minutes

Serving: 1

Ingredients:

- 2 basics cooked chaffles
- Cooking spray
- 2 slices bacon
- 1 egg

Method:

1. Spray your pan with oil.
2. Place it over medium heat.
3. Cook the bacon until golden and crispy.
4. Put the bacon on top of one chaffle.
5. In the same pan, cook the egg without mixing until the yolk is set.
6. Add the egg on top of the bacon.
7. Top with another chaffle.

Nutritional Value:

- Calories 514
- Total Fat 47 g
- Saturated Fat 27 g
- Cholesterol 274 mg
- Sodium 565 mg
- Potassium 106 mg
- Total Carbohydrate 2 g
- Dietary Fiber 1 g
- Protein 21 g
- Total Sugars 1 g

RECIPES

Beginners

Chocolate Melt Chaffles
Preparation Time: 15 minutes
Cooking Time: 36 minutes
Servings: 4

Ingredients

For the chaffles:

- 2 eggs, beaten
- ¼ cup finely grated Gruyere cheese
- 2 tbsp heavy cream
- 1 tbsp coconut flour
- 2 tbsp cream cheese, softened
- 3 tbsp unsweetened cocoa powder
- 2 tsp vanilla extract
- A pinch of salt

For the chocolate sauce:

- 1/3 cup + 1 tbsp heavy cream
- 1 ½ oz unsweetened baking chocolate, chopped
- 1 ½ tsp sugar-free maple syrup
- 1 ½ tsp vanilla extract

Directions:

For the chaffles:

1. Preheat the waffle iron.
2. In a medium bowl, mix all the ingredients for the chaffles.
3. Open the iron and add a quarter of the mixture. Close and cook until crispy, 7 minutes.
4. Transfer the chaffle to a plate and make 3 more with the remaining batter.

For the chocolate sauce:

1. Pour the heavy cream into saucepan and simmer over low heat, 3 minutes.
2. Turn the heat off and add the chocolate. Allow melting for a few minutes and stir until fully melted, 5 minutes.
3. Mix in the maple syrup and vanilla extract.
4. Assemble the chaffles in layers with the chocolate sauce sandwiched between each layer.
5. Slice and serve immediately.

Nutrition:
Calories 172
Fats 13.57g
Carbs 6.65g
Net Carbs 3.65g
Protein 5.76g

Chaffles with Keto Ice Cream

Preparation Time: 10 minutes
Cooking Time: 14 minutes
Servings: 2

Ingredients:

- 1 egg, beaten
- ½ cup finely grated mozzarella cheese
- ¼ cup almond flour
- 2 tbsp swerve confectioner's sugar
- 1/8 tsp xanthan gum
- Low-carb ice cream (flavor of your choice) for serving

Directions:

1. Preheat the waffle iron.
2. In a medium bowl, mix all the ingredients except the ice cream.
3. Open the iron and add half of the mixture. Close and cook until crispy, 7 minutes.
4. Transfer the chaffle to a plate and make second one with the remaining batter.
5. On each chaffle, add a scoop of low carb ice cream, fold into half-moons and enjoy.

Nutrition:
Calories 89
Fats 6.48g
Carbs 1.67g

Net Carbs 1.37g
Protein 5.91g

Strawberry Shortcake Chaffle Bowls

Preparation Time: 10 minutes
Cooking Time: 28 minutes
Servings: 4

Ingredients:

- 1 egg, beaten
- ½ cup finely grated mozzarella cheese
- 1 tbsp almond flour
- ¼ tsp baking powder
- 2 drops cake batter extract
- 1 cup cream cheese, softened
- 1 cup fresh strawberries, sliced
- 1 tbsp sugar-free maple syrup

Directions:

1. Preheat a waffle bowl maker and grease lightly with cooking spray.
2. Meanwhile, in a medium bowl, whisk all the ingredients except the cream cheese and strawberries.
3. Open the iron, pour in half of the mixture, cover, and cook until crispy, 6 to 7 minutes.
4. Remove the chaffle bowl onto a plate and set aside.
5. Make a second chaffle bowl with the remaining batter.
6. To serve, divide the cream cheese into the chaffle bowls and top with the strawberries.
7. Drizzle the filling with the maple syrup and serve.

Nutrition:

Calories 235
Fats 20.62g
Carbs 5.9g
Net Carbs 5g
Protein 7.51g

Chaffles with Raspberry Syrup

Preparation Time: 10 minutes
Cooking Time: 38 minutes
Servings: 4

Ingredients:

For the chaffles:

- 1 egg, beaten
- ½ cup finely shredded cheddar cheese
- 1 tsp almond flour
- 1 tsp sour cream

For the raspberry syrup:

- 1 cup fresh raspberries
- ¼ cup swerve sugar
- ¼ cup water
- 1 tsp vanilla extract

Directions:

For the chaffles:

1. Preheat the waffle iron.
2. Meanwhile, in a medium bowl, mix the egg, cheddar cheese, almond flour, and sour cream.
3. Open the iron, pour in half of the mixture, cover, and cook until crispy, 7 minutes.
4. Remove the chaffle onto a plate and make another with the remaining batter.

For the raspberry syrup:

1. Meanwhile, add the raspberries, swerve sugar, water, and vanilla extract to a medium pot. Set over low heat and cook until the raspberries soften and sugar becomes syrupy. Occasionally stir while mashing the raspberries as you go. Turn the heat off when your desired consistency is achieved and set aside to cool.
2. Drizzle some syrup on the chaffles and enjoy when ready.

Nutrition:
Calories 105
Fats 7.11g
Carbs 4.31g
Net Carbs 2.21g
Protein 5.83g

Chaffle Cannoli
Preparation Time: 15 minutes
Cooking Time: 28 minutes
Servings: 4

Ingredients:

For the chaffles:

- 1 large egg
- 1 egg yolk
- 3 tbsp butter, melted
- 1 tbso swerve confectioner's
- 1 cup finely grated Parmesan cheese
- 2 tbsp finely grated mozzarella cheese

For the cannoli filling:

- ½ cup ricotta cheese
- 2 tbsp swerve confectioner's sugar
- 1 tsp vanilla extract
- 2 tbsp unsweetened chocolate chips for garnishing

Directions:

1. Preheat the waffle iron.
2. Meanwhile, in a medium bowl, mix all the ingredients for the chaffles.
3. Open the iron, pour in a quarter of the mixture, cover, and cook until crispy, 7 minutes.
4. Remove the chaffle onto a plate and make 3 more with the remaining batter.
5. Meanwhile, for the cannoli filling:
6. Beat the ricotta cheese and swerve confectioner's sugar until smooth. Mix in the vanilla.
7. On each chaffle, spread some of the filling and wrap over.
8. Garnish the creamy ends with some chocolate chips.
9. Serve immediately.

Nutrition:
Calories 308
Fats 25.05g
Carbs 5.17g
Net Carbs 5.17g
Protein 15.18g

Blueberry Chaffles

Preparation Time: 10 minutes
Cooking Time: 28 minutes
Servings: 4

Ingredients:

- 1 egg, beaten
- ½ cup finely grated mozzarella cheese
- 1 tbsp cream cheese, softened
- 1 tbsp sugar-free maple syrup + extra for topping
- ½ cup blueberries
- ¼ tsp vanilla extract

Directions:

1. Preheat the waffle iron.
2. In a medium bowl, mix all the ingredients.
3. Open the iron, lightly grease with cooking spray and pour in a quarter of the mixture.
4. Close the iron and cook until golden brown and crispy, 7 minutes.
5. Remove the chaffle onto a plate and set aside.
6. Make the remaining chaffles with the remaining mixture.
7. Drizzle the chaffles with maple syrup and serve afterward.

Nutrition:

Calories 137
Fats 9.07g
Carbs 4.02g

Net Carbs 3.42g
Protein 9.59g

Nutter Butter Chaffles

Preparation Time: 15 minutes
Cooking Time: 14 minutes
Servings: 2

Ingredients:

For the chaffles:

- 2 tbsp sugar-free peanut butter powder
- 2 tbsp maple (sugar-free) syrup
- 1 egg, beaten
- ¼ cup finely grated mozzarella cheese
- ¼ tsp baking powder
- ¼ tsp almond butter
- ¼ tsp peanut butter extract
- 1 tbsp softened cream cheese

For the frosting:

- ½ cup almond flour
- 1 cup peanut butter
- 3 tbsp almond milk
- ½ tsp vanilla extract
- ½ cup maple (sugar-free) syrup

Directions:

1. Preheat the waffle iron.
2. Meanwhile, in a medium bowl, mix all the ingredients until smooth.
3. Open the iron and pour in half of the mixture.
4. Close the iron and cook until crispy, 6 to 7 minutes.
5. Remove the chaffle onto a plate and set aside.
6. Make a second chaffle with the remaining batter.
7. While the chaffles cool, make the frosting.
8. Pour the almond flour in a medium saucepan and stir-fry over medium heat until golden.
9. Transfer the almond flour to a blender and top with the remaining frosting ingredients. Process until smooth.

10. Spread the frosting on the chaffles and serve afterward.

Nutrition:

Calories 239
Fats 15.48g
Carbs 17.42g
Net Carbs 15.92g
Protein 7.52g

Chaffled Brownie Sundae

Preparation Time: 12 minutes
Cooking Time: 30 minutes
Servings: 4

Ingredients:

For the chaffles:

- 2 eggs, beaten
- 1 tbsp unsweetened cocoa powder
- 1 tbsp erythritol
- 1 cup finely grated mozzarella cheese

For the topping:

- 3 tbsp unsweetened chocolate, chopped
- 3 tbsp unsalted butter
- ½ cup swerve sugar
- Low-carb ice cream for topping
- 1 cup whipped cream for topping
- 3 tbsp sugar-free caramel sauce

Directions:

For the chaffles:

1. Preheat the waffle iron.
2. Meanwhile, in a medium bowl, mix all the ingredients for the chaffles.
3. Open the iron, pour in a quarter of the mixture, cover, and cook until crispy, 7 minutes.
4. Remove the chaffle onto a plate and make 3 more with the remaining batter.
5. Plate and set aside.

For the topping:

1. Meanwhile, melt the chocolate and butter in a medium saucepan with occasional stirring, 2 minutes.

To Servings:

1. Divide the chaffles into wedges and top with the ice cream, whipped cream, and swirl the chocolate sauce and caramel sauce on top.
2. Serve immediately.

Nutrition:
Calories 165
Fats 11.39g
Carbs 3.81g
Net Carbs 2.91g
Protein 12.79g

Brie and Blackberry Chaffles

Preparation Time: 15 minutes
Cooking Time: 36 minutes
Servings: 4

Ingredients:

For the chaffles:

- 2 eggs, beaten
- 1 cup finely grated mozzarella cheese
- For the topping:
- 1 ½ cups blackberries
- 1 lemon, 1 tsp zest and 2 tbsp juice
- 1 tbsp erythritol
- 4 slices Brie cheese

Directions:

For the chaffles:

1. Preheat the waffle iron.
2. Meanwhile, in a medium bowl, mix the eggs and mozzarella cheese.
3. Open the iron, pour in a quarter of the mixture, cover, and cook until crispy, 7 minutes.
4. Remove the chaffle onto a plate and make 3 more with the remaining batter.
5. Plate and set aside.

For the topping:

1. In a medium pot, add the blackberries, lemon zest, lemon juice, and erythritol. Cook until the blackberries break and the sauce thickens, 5 minutes. Turn the heat off.
2. Arrange the chaffles on the baking sheet and place two Brie cheese slices on each. Top with blackberry mixture and transfer the baking sheet to the oven.
3. Bake until the cheese melts, 2 to 3 minutes.
4. Remove from the oven, allow cooling and serve afterward.

Nutrition:

Calories 576
Fats 42.22g
Carbs 7.07g
Net Carbs 3.67g
Protein 42.35g

Carrot Chaffle Cake

Preparation Time: 15 minutes
Cooking Time: 24 minutes
Servings: 6

Ingredients:

- 1 egg, beaten
- 2 tablespoons melted butter
- ½ cup carrot, shredded
- ¾ cup almond flour
- 1 teaspoon baking powder
- 2 tablespoons heavy whipping cream
- 2 tablespoons sweetener
- 1 tablespoon walnuts, chopped
- 1 teaspoon pumpkin spice
- 2 teaspoons cinnamon

Directions:

1. Preheat your waffle maker.
2. In a large bowl, combine all the ingredients.
3. Pour some of the mixture into the waffle maker.
4. Close and cook for 4 minutes.
5. Repeat steps until all the remaining batter has been used.

Nutrition:

Calories 294
Total Fat 26.7g
Saturated Fat 12g
Cholesterol 133mg
Sodium 144mg
Potassium 421mg
Total Carbohydrate 11.6g
Dietary Fiber 4.5g
Protein 6.8g
Total Sugars 1.7g

Cereal Chaffle Cake

Preparation Time: 5 minutes
Cooking Time: 8 minutes
Servings: 2

Ingredients:

- 1 egg
- 2 tablespoons almond flour
- ½ teaspoon coconut flour
- 1 tablespoon melted butter
- 1 tablespoon cream cheese
- 1 tablespoon plain cereal, crushed
- ¼ teaspoon vanilla extract
- ¼ teaspoon baking powder
- 1 tablespoon sweetener
- 1/8 teaspoon xanthan gum

Directions:

1. Plug in your waffle maker to preheat.
2. Add all the ingredients in a large bowl.
3. Mix until well blended.
4. Let the batter rest for 2 minutes before cooking.
5. Pour half of the mixture into the waffle maker.
6. Seal and cook for 4 minutes.
7. Make the next chaffle using the same steps.

Nutrition:

Calories154
Total Fat 21.2g
Saturated Fat 10 g
Cholesterol 113.3mg
Sodium 96.9mg
Potassium 453 mg
Total Carbohydrate 5.9g
Dietary Fiber 1.7g
Protein 4.6g
Total Sugars 2.7g

Ham, Cheese & Tomato Chaffle Sandwich

Preparation Time: 5 minutes
Cooking Time: 10 minutes
Servings: 2

Ingredients:

- 1 teaspoon olive oil
- 2 slices ham
- 4 basic chaffles
- 1 tablespoon mayonnaise
- 2 slices Provolone cheese
- 1 tomato, sliced

Directions:

1. Add the olive oil to a pan over medium heat.
2. Cook the ham for 1 minute per side.
3. Spread the chaffles with mayonnaise.
4. Top with the ham, cheese and tomatoes.
5. Top with another chaffle to make a sandwich.

Nutrition:

Calories 198
Total Fat 14.7g
Saturated Fat 6.3g
Cholesterol 37mg
Sodium 664mg

Total Carbohydrate 4.6g
Dietary Fiber 0.7g
Total Sugars 1.5g
Protein 12.2g
Potassium 193mg

Broccoli & Cheese Chaffle

Preparation Time: 5 minutes
Cooking Time: 8 minutes
Servings: 2

Ingredients:

- ¼ cup broccoli florets
- 1 egg, beaten
- 1 tablespoon almond flour
- ¼ teaspoon garlic powder
- ½ cup cheddar cheese

Directions:

1. Preheat your waffle maker.
2. Add the broccoli to the food processor.
3. Pulse until chopped.
4. Add to a bowl.
5. Stir in the egg and the rest of the ingredients.
6. Mix well.
7. Pour half of the batter to the waffle maker.
8. Cover and cook for 4 minutes.
9. Repeat procedure to make the next chaffle.

Nutrition:

Calories 170
Total Fat 13 g
Saturated Fat 7 g
Cholesterol 112 mg
Sodium 211 mg

Potassium 94 mg
Total Carbohydrate 2 g
Dietary Fiber 1 g
Protein 11 g
Total Sugars 1 g

Chaffle with Sausage Gravy

Preparation Time: 5 minutes
Cooking Time: 15 minutes
Servings: 2

Ingredients:

- ¼ cup sausage, cooked
- 3 tablespoons chicken broth
- 2 teaspoons cream cheese
- 2 tablespoons heavy whipping cream
- ¼ teaspoon garlic powder
- Pepper to taste
- 2 basic chaffles

Directions:

1. Add the sausage, broth, cream cheese, cream, garlic powder and pepper to a pan over medium heat.
2. Bring to a boil and then reduce heat.
3. Simmer for 10 minutes or until the sauce has thickened.
4. Pour the gravy on top of the basic chaffles
5. Serve.

Nutrition:

Calories 212
Total Fat 17 g
Saturated Fat 10 g
Cholesterol 134 mg
Sodium 350 mg
Potassium 133 mg
Total Carbohydrate 3 g
Dietary Fiber 1 g
Protein 11 g
Total Sugars 1 g

Barbecue Chaffle

Preparation Time: 5 minutes
Cooking Time: 8 minutes
Servings: 2

Ingredients:

- 1 egg, beaten
- ½ cup cheddar cheese, shredded
- ½ teaspoon barbecue sauce
- ¼ teaspoon baking powder

Directions:

1. Plug in your waffle maker to preheat.
2. Mix all the ingredients in a bowl.
3. Pour half of the mixture to your waffle maker.
4. Cover and cook for 4 minutes.
5. Repeat the same steps for the next barbecue chaffle.

Nutrition:

Calories 295
Total Fat 23 g
Saturated Fat 13 g
Cholesterol 223 mg
Sodium 414 mg

Potassium 179 mg
Total Carbohydrate 2 g
Dietary Fiber 1 g
Protein 20 g
Total Sugars 1 g

Bacon & Chicken Ranch Chaffle

Preparation Time: 5 minutes
Cooking Time: 8 minutes
Servings: 2

Ingredients:

- 1 egg
- ¼ cup chicken cubes, cooked
- 1 slice bacon, cooked and chopped
- ¼ cup cheddar cheese, shredded
- 1 teaspoon ranch dressing powder

Directions:

1. Preheat your waffle maker.
2. In a bowl, mix all the ingredients.
3. Add half of the mixture to your waffle maker.
4. Cover and cook for 4 minutes.
5. Make the second chaffle using the same steps.

Nutrition:

Calories 200
Total Fat 14 g
Saturated Fat 6 g
Cholesterol 129 mg
Sodium 463 mg

Potassium 130 mg
Total Carbohydrate 2 g
Dietary Fiber 1 g
Protein 16 g
Total Sugars 1 g

Pumpkin & Pecan Chaffle

Preparation Time: 5 minutes
Cooking Time: 10 minutes
Servings: 2

Ingredients:

- 1 egg, beaten
- ½ cup mozzarella cheese, grated
- ½ teaspoon pumpkin spice
- 1 tablespoon pureed pumpkin
- 2 tablespoons almond flour
- 1 teaspoon sweetener
- 2 tablespoons pecans, chopped

Directions:

1. Turn on the waffle maker.
2. Beat the egg in a bowl.
3. Stir in the rest of the ingredients.
4. Pour half of the mixture into the device.
5. Seal the lid.
6. Cook for 5 minutes.
7. Remove the chaffle carefully.
8. Repeat the steps to make the second chaffle.

Nutrition:

Calories 210
Total Fat 17 g
Saturated Fat 10 g
Cholesterol 110 mg
Sodium 250 mg
Potassium 570 mg
Total Carbohydrate 4.6 g
Dietary Fiber 1.7 g
Protein 11 g
Total Sugars 2 g

Cheeseburger Chaffle

Preparation Time: 15 minutes
Cooking Time: 15 minutes
Servings: 2

Ingredients:

- 1 lb. ground beef
- 1 onion, minced
- 1 tsp. parsley, chopped
- 1 egg, beaten
- Salt and pepper to taste
- 1 tablespoon olive oil
- 4 basic chaffles
- 2 lettuce leaves
- 2 cheese slices
- 1 tablespoon dill pickles
- Ketchup
- Mayonnaise

Directions:

1. In a large bowl, combine the ground beef, onion, parsley, egg, salt and pepper.
2. Mix well.
3. Form 2 thick patties.
4. Add olive oil to the pan.
5. Place the pan over medium heat.
6. Cook the patty for 3 to 5 minutes per side or until fully cooked.
7. Place the patty on top of each chaffle.
8. Top with lettuce, cheese and pickles.
9. Squirt ketchup and mayo over the patty and veggies.
10. Top with another chaffle.

Nutrition:

Calories 325
Total Fat 16.3g
Saturated Fat 6.5g
Cholesterol 157mg

Sodium 208mg
Total Carbohydrate 3g
Dietary Fiber 0.7g
Total Sugars 1.4g
Protein 39.6g
Potassium 532mg

Double Choco Chaffle

Preparation Time: 5 minutes
Cooking Time: 10 minutes
Servings: 2

Ingredients:

- 1 egg
- 2 teaspoons coconut flour
- 2 tablespoons sweetener
- 1 tablespoon cocoa powder
- ¼ teaspoon baking powder
- 1 oz. cream cheese
- ½ teaspoon vanilla
- 1 tablespoon sugar-free chocolate chips

Directions:

1. Put all the ingredients in a large bowl.
2. Mix well.
3. Pour half of the mixture into the waffle maker.
4. Seal the device.
5. Cook for 4 minutes.
6. Uncover and transfer to a plate to cool.
7. Repeat the procedure to make the second chaffle.

Nutrition:
Calories 171
Total Fat 10.7g
Saturated Fat 5.3g
Cholesterol 97mg
Sodium 106mg
Potassium 179mg
Total Carbohydrate 3g
Dietary Fiber 4.8g
Protein 5.8g
Total Sugars 0.4g

Cream Cheese Chaffle

Preparation Time: 5 minutes
Cooking Time: 8 minutes
Servings: 2

Ingredients:

- 1 egg, beaten
- 1 oz. cream cheese
- ½ teaspoon vanilla
- 4 teaspoons sweetener
- ¼ teaspoon baking powder
- Cream cheese

Directions:

1. Preheat your waffle maker.
2. Add all the ingredients in a bowl.
3. Mix well.
4. Pour half of the batter into the waffle maker.
5. Seal the device.
6. Cook for 4 minutes.
7. Remove the chaffle from the waffle maker.
8. Make the second one using the same steps.
9. Spread remaining cream cheese on top before serving.

Nutrition:

Calories 169
Total Fat 14.3g
Saturated Fat 7.6g
Cholesterol 195mg
Sodium 147mg
Potassium 222mg
Total Carbohydrate 4g
Dietary Fiber 4g
Protein 7.7g
Total Sugars 0.7g

Intermediate

41. Chaffle Fruit Snacks

Preparation Time: 10 minutes
Cooking Time: 14 minutes
Servings: 2

Ingredients:

- 1 egg, beaten
- ½ cup finely grated cheddar cheese
- ½ cup Greek yogurt for topping
- 8 raspberries and blackberries for topping

Directions:

1. Preheat the waffle iron.
2. Mix the egg and cheddar cheese in a medium bowl.
3. Open the iron and add half of the mixture. Close and cook until crispy, 7 minutes.
4. Remove the chaffle onto a plate and make another with the remaining mixture.
5. Cut each chaffle into wedges and arrange on a plate.
6. Top each waffle with a tablespoon of yogurt and then two berries.
7. Serve afterward.

Nutrition:

Calories 207
Fats 15.29g
Carbs 4.36g

Net Carbs 3.86g
Protein 12.91g

Keto Belgian Sugar Chaffles

Preparation Time: 10 minutes
Cooking Time: 24 minutes
Servings: 4

Ingredients:

- 1 egg, beaten
- 2 tbsp swerve brown sugar
- ½ tbsp butter, melted
- 1 tsp vanilla extract
- 1 cup finely grated Parmesan cheese

Directions:
1. Preheat the waffle iron.
2. Mix all the ingredients in a medium bowl.
3. Open the iron and pour in a quarter of the mixture. Close and cook until crispy, 6 minutes.
4. Remove the chaffle onto a plate and make 3 more with the remaining ingredients.
5. Cut each chaffle into wedges, plate, allow cooling and serve.

Nutrition:
Calories 136

Fats 9.45g

Carbs 3.69g

Net Carbs 3.69g

Protein 8.5g

Lemon and Paprika Chaffles
Preparation Time: 10 minutes

Cooking Time: 28 minutes

Servings: 4

Ingredients:
- 1 egg, beaten
- 1 oz cream cheese, softened
- 1/3 cup finely grated mozzarella cheese
- 1 tbsp almond flour
- 1 tsp butter, melted
- 1 tsp maple (sugar-free) syrup
- ½ tsp sweet paprika
- ½ tsp lemon extract

Directions:
1. Preheat the waffle iron.
2. Mix all the ingredients in a medium bowl
3. Open the iron and pour in a quarter of the mixture. Close and cook until crispy, 7 minutes.
4. Remove the chaffle onto a plate and make 3 more with the remaining mixture.

5. Cut each chaffle into wedges, plate, allow cooling and serve.

Nutrition:

Calories 48

Fats 4.22g

Carbs 0.6g

Net Carbs 0.5g

Protein 2g

Herby Chaffle Snacks

Preparation Time: 10 minutes

Cooking Time: 28 minutes

Servings: 4

Ingredients:

- 1 egg, beaten
- ½ cup finely grated Monterey Jack cheese
- ¼ cup finely grated Parmesan cheese
- ½ tsp dried mixed herbs

Directions:

1. Preheat the waffle iron.
2. Mix all the ingredients in a medium bowl
3. Open the iron and pour in a quarter of the mixture. Close and cook until crispy, 7 minutes.
4. Remove the chaffle onto a plate and make 3 more with the rest of the ingredients.
5. Cut each chaffle into wedges and plate.
6. Allow cooling and serve.

Nutrition:

Calories 96

Fats 6.29g

Carbs 2.19g

Net Carbs 2.19g

Protein 7.42g

Pumpkin Spice Chaffles

Preparation Time: 10 minutes
Cooking Time: 14 minutes
Servings: 2

Ingredients:

- 1 egg, beaten
- ½ tsp pumpkin pie spice
- ½ cup finely grated mozzarella cheese
- 1 tbsp sugar-free pumpkin puree

Directions:

1. Preheat the waffle iron.
2. In a medium bowl, mix all the ingredients.
3. Open the iron, pour in half of the batter, close, and cook until crispy, 6 to 7 minutes.
4. Remove the chaffle onto a plate and set aside.
5. Make another chaffle with the remaining batter.
6. Allow cooling and serve afterward.

Nutrition:

Calories 90
Fats 6.46g
Carbs 1.98g
Net Carbs 1.58g
Protein 5.94g

Breakfast Spinach Ricotta Chaffles

Preparation Time: 10 minutes
Cooking Time: 28 minutes
Servings: 4

Ingredients:

- 4 oz frozen spinach, thawed, squeezed dry
- 1 cup ricotta cheese
- 2 eggs, beaten
- ½ tsp garlic powder
- ¼ cup finely grated Pecorino Romano cheese
- ½ cup finely grated mozzarella cheese
- Salt and freshly ground black pepper to taste

Directions:

1. Preheat the waffle iron.
2. In a medium bowl, mix all the ingredients.
3. Open the iron, lightly grease with cooking spray and spoon in a quarter of the mixture.
4. Close the iron and cook until brown and crispy, 7 minutes.
5. Remove the chaffle onto a plate and set aside.
6. Make three more chaffles with the remaining mixture.
7. Allow cooling and serve afterward.

Nutrition:

Calories 188
Fats 13.15g
Carbs 5.06g

Net Carbs 4.06g
Protein 12.79g

Scrambled Egg Stuffed Chaffles

Preparation Time: 15 minutes
Cooking Time: 28 minutes
Servings: 4

Ingredients:

For the chaffles:

- 1 cup finely grated cheddar cheese
- 2 eggs, beaten
- For the egg stuffing:
- 1 tbsp olive oil

- 1 small red bell pepper
- 4 large eggs
- 1 small green bell pepper
- Salt and freshly ground black pepper to taste
- 2 tbsp grated Parmesan cheese

Directions:

For the chaffles:

1. Preheat the waffle iron.
2. In a medium bowl, mix the cheddar cheese and egg.
3. Open the iron, pour in a quarter of the mixture, close, and cook until crispy, 6 to 7 minutes.
4. Plate and make three more chaffles using the remaining mixture.

For the egg stuffing:

1. Meanwhile, heat the olive oil in a medium skillet over medium heat on a stovetop.
2. In a medium bowl, beat the eggs with the bell peppers, salt, black pepper, and Parmesan cheese.
3. Pour the mixture into the skillet and scramble until set to your likeness, 2 minutes.
4. Between two chaffles, spoon half of the scrambled eggs and repeat with the second set of chaffles.
5. Serve afterward.

Nutrition Facts per Serving:
Calories 387
Fats 22.52g
Carbs 18.12g
Net Carbs 17.52g
Protein 27.76g

Mixed Berry-Vanilla Chaffles

Preparation Time: 10 minutes
Cooking Time: 28 minutes
Servings: 4

Ingredients:

- 1 egg, beaten
- ½ cup finely grated mozzarella cheese
- 1 tbsp cream cheese, softened
- 1 tbsp sugar-free maple syrup
- 2 strawberries, sliced
- 2 raspberries, slices
- ¼ tsp blackberry extract
- ¼ tsp vanilla extract
- ½ cup plain yogurt for serving

Directions:

1. Preheat the waffle iron.
2. In a medium bowl, mix all the ingredients except the yogurt.
3. Open the iron, lightly grease with cooking spray and pour in a quarter of the mixture.
4. Close the iron and cook until golden brown and crispy, 7 minutes.
5. Remove the chaffle onto a plate and set aside.
6. Make three more chaffles with the remaining mixture.
7. To Servings: top with the yogurt and enjoy.

Nutrition Facts per Serving:

Calories 78
Fats 5.29g
Carbs 3.02g
Net Carbs 2.72g
Protein 4.32g

Ham and Cheddar Chaffles

Preparation Time: 15 minutes
Cooking Time: 28 minutes
Servings: 4

Ingredients:

- 1 cup finely shredded parsnips, steamed
- 8 oz ham, diced
- 2 eggs, beaten
- 1 ½ cups finely grated cheddar cheese
- ½ tsp garlic powder
- 2 tbsp chopped fresh parsley leaves
- ¼ tsp smoked paprika
- ½ tsp dried thyme
- Salt and freshly ground black pepper to taste

Directions:

1. Preheat the waffle iron.
2. In a medium bowl, mix all the ingredients.
3. Open the iron, lightly grease with cooking spray and pour in a quarter of the mixture.
4. Close the iron and cook until crispy, 7 minutes.
5. Remove the chaffle onto a plate and set aside.
6. Make three more chaffles using the remaining mixture.
7. Serve afterward.

Nutrition Facts per Serving:

Calories 506
Fats 24.05g
Carbs 30.02g
Net Carbs 28.22g
Protein 42.74g

Savory Gruyere and Chives Chaffles
Preparation Time: 15 minutes
Cooking Time: 14 minutes
Servings: 2
Ingredients:

- 2 eggs, beaten
- 1 cup finely grated Gruyere cheese
- 2 tbsp finely grated cheddar cheese
- 1/8 tsp freshly ground black pepper
- 3 tbsp minced fresh chives + more for garnishing
- 2 sunshine fried eggs for topping

Directions:
1. Preheat the waffle iron.
2. In a medium bowl, mix the eggs, cheeses, black pepper, and chives.
3. Open the iron and pour in half of the mixture.
4. Close the iron and cook until brown and crispy, 7 minutes.
5. Remove the chaffle onto a plate and set aside.
6. Make another chaffle using the remaining mixture.
7. Top each chaffle with one fried egg each, garnish with the chives and serve.

Nutrition Facts per Serving:
Calories 712
Fats 41.32g
Carbs 3.88g
Net Carbs 3.78g
Protein 23.75g

Chicken Quesadilla Chaffle
Preparation Time: 10 minutes
Cooking Time: 14 minutes
Servings: 2
Ingredients:

- 1 egg, beaten
- ¼ tsp taco seasoning
- 1/3 cup finely grated cheddar cheese
- 1/3 cup cooked chopped chicken

<u>Directions:</u>

1. Preheat the waffle iron.
2. In a medium bowl, mix the eggs, taco seasoning, and cheddar cheese. Add the chicken and combine well.
3. Open the iron, lightly grease with cooking spray and pour in half of the mixture.
4. Close the iron and cook until brown and crispy, 7 minutes.
5. Remove the chaffle onto a plate and set aside.
6. Make another chaffle using the remaining mixture.
7. Serve afterward.

<u>Nutrition Facts per Serving:</u>
Calories 314
Fats 20.64g
Carbs 5.71g
Net Carbs 5.71g
Protein 16.74g

Hot Chocolate Breakfast Chaffle

Preparation Time: 10 minutes
Cooking Time: 14 minutes
Servings: 2

Ingredients:

- 1 egg, beaten
- 2 tbsp almond flour
- 1 tbsp unsweetened cocoa powder
- 2 tbsp cream cheese, softened
- ¼ cup finely grated Monterey Jack cheese
- 2 tbsp sugar-free maple syrup
- 1 tsp vanilla extract

Directions:

1. Preheat the waffle iron.
2. In a medium bowl, mix all the ingredients.
3. Open the iron, lightly grease with cooking spray and pour in half of the mixture.
4. Close the iron and cook until crispy, 7 minutes.
5. Remove the chaffle onto a plate and set aside.
6. Pour the remaining batter in the iron and make the second chaffle.
7. Allow cooling and serve afterward.

Nutrition Facts per Serving:

Calories 47
Fats 3.67g
Carbs 1.39g

Net Carbs 0.89g
Protein 2.29g

Blueberry Chaffles

Preparation Time: 15 minutes

Servings: 4

Ingredients:

- 2 eggs
- 1/2 cup blueberries
- 1/2 tsp baking powder
- 1/2 tsp vanilla
- 2 tsp Swerve
- 3 tbsp almond flour
- 1 cup mozzarella cheese, shredded

Directions:

1. Preheat your waffle maker.
2. In a medium bowl, mix eggs, vanilla, Swerve, almond flour, and cheese.
3. Add blueberries and stir well.
4. Spray waffle maker with cooking spray.
5. Pour 1/4 batter in the hot waffle maker and cook for 5-8 minutes or until golden brown. Repeat with the remaining batter.
6. Serve and enjoy.

Nutrition:

Calories 96

Fat 6.1 g

Carbohydrates 5.7 g

Sugar 2.2 g

Protein 6.1 g

Cholesterol 86 mg

Pecan Pumpkin Chaffle

Preparation Time: 15 minutes
Servings: 2

Ingredients:

- 1 egg
- 2 tbsp pecans, toasted and chopped
- 2 tbsp almond flour
- 1 tsp erythritol
- 1/4 tsp pumpkin pie spice
- 1 tbsp pumpkin puree
- 1/2 cup mozzarella cheese, grated

Directions:

1. Preheat your waffle maker.
2. Beat egg in a small bowl.
3. Add remaining ingredients and mix well.
4. Spray waffle maker with cooking spray.
5. Pour half batter in the hot waffle maker and cook for 5 minutes or until golden brown. Repeat with the remaining batter.
6. Serve and enjoy.

Nutrition:

Calories 121
Fat 9.7 g
Carbohydrates 5.7 g

Sugar 3.3 g
Protein 6.7 g
Cholesterol 86 mg

Pumpkin Cheesecake Chaffle

Preparation Time: 15 minutes

Servings: 2

Ingredients:

For chaffle:

- 1 egg
- 1/2 tsp vanilla
- 1/2 tsp baking powder, gluten-free
- 1/4 tsp pumpkin spice
- 1 tsp cream cheese, softened
- 2 tsp heavy cream
- 1 tbsp Swerve
- 1 tbsp almond flour
- 2 tsp pumpkin puree
- 1/2 cup mozzarella cheese, shredded

For filling:

- 1/4 tsp vanilla
- 1 tbsp Swerve
- 2 tbsp cream cheese

Directions:

1. Preheat your mini waffle maker.
2. In a small bowl, mix all chaffle ingredients.
3. Spray waffle maker with cooking spray.
4. Pour half batter in the hot waffle maker and cook for 3-5 minutes. Repeat with the remaining batter.
5. In a small bowl, combine all filling ingredients.
6. Spread filling mixture between two chaffles and place in the fridge for 10 minutes.
7. Serve and enjoy.

Nutrition:
Calories 107
Fat 7.2 g
Carbohydrates 5 g
Sugar 0.7 g
Protein 6.7 g
Cholesterol 93 mg

Quick & Easy Blueberry Chaffle

Preparation Time: 15 minutes
Servings: 2

Ingredients:

- 1 egg, lightly beaten
- 1/4 cup blueberries
- 1/2 tsp vanilla
- 1 oz cream cheese
- 1/4 tsp baking powder, gluten-free
- 4 tsp Swerve
- 1 tbsp coconut flour

Directions:

1. Preheat your waffle maker.
2. In a small bowl, mix coconut flour, baking powder, and Swerve until well combined.
3. Add vanilla, cream cheese, egg, and vanilla and whisk until combined.
4. Spray waffle maker with cooking spray.
5. Pour half batter in the hot waffle maker and top with 4-5 blueberries and cook for 4-5 minutes until golden brown. Repeat with the remaining batter.
6. Serve and enjoy.

Nutrition:

Calories 135
Fat 8.2 g
Carbohydrates 11 g

Sugar 2.6 g
Protein 5 g
Cholesterol 97 mg

Apple Cinnamon Chaffles

Preparation Time: 20 minutes

Servings: 3

Ingredients:

- 3 eggs, lightly beaten
- 1 cup mozzarella cheese, shredded
- ¼ cup apple, chopped
- ½ tsp monk fruit sweetener
- 1 ½ tsp cinnamon
- ¼ tsp baking powder, gluten-free
- 2 tbsp coconut flour

Directions:

1. Preheat your waffle maker.
2. Add remaining ingredients and stir until well combined.
3. Spray waffle maker with cooking spray.
4. Pour 1/3 of batter in the hot waffle maker and cook for 4 minutes or until golden brown. Repeat with the remaining batter.
5. Serve and enjoy.

Nutrition:

Calories 142

Fat 7.4 g

Carbohydrates 9.7 g

Sugar 3 g

Protein 9.6 g

Cholesterol 169 mg

Cinnamon Cream Cheese Chaffle

Preparation Time: 15 minutes

Servings: 2

Ingredients:

- 2 eggs, lightly beaten
- 1 tsp collagen
- ¼ tsp baking powder, gluten-free
- 1 tsp monk fruit sweetener
- ½ tsp cinnamon
- ¼ cup cream cheese, softened
- Pinch of salt

Directions:

1. Preheat your waffle maker.
2. Add all ingredients into the bowl and beat using hand mixer until well combined.
3. Spray waffle maker with cooking spray.
4. Pour 1/2 batter in the hot waffle maker and cook for 3-4 minutes or until golden brown. Repeat with the remaining batter.
5. Serve and enjoy.

Nutrition:

Calories 179

Fat 14.5 g

Carbohydrates 1.9 g

Sugar 0.4 g

Protein 10.8 g

Cholesterol 196 mg

Mozzarella Peanut Butter Chaffle

Preparation Time: 15 minutes
Servings: 2

Ingredients:

- 1 egg, lightly beaten
- 2 tbsp peanut butter
- 2 tbsp Swerve
- 1/2 cup mozzarella cheese, shredded

Directions:

1. Preheat your waffle maker.
2. In a bowl, mix egg, cheese, Swerve, and peanut butter until well combined.
3. Spray waffle maker with cooking spray.
4. Pour half batter in the hot waffle maker and cook for 4 minutes or until golden brown. Repeat with the remaining batter.
5. Serve and enjoy.

Nutrition:
Calories 150
Fat 11.5 g
Carbohydrates 5.6 g
Sugar 1.7 g
Protein 8.8 g
Cholesterol 86 mg

Choco Chip Pumpkin Chaffle

Preparation Time: 15 minutes

Servings: 2

Ingredients:

- 1 egg, lightly beaten
- 1 tbsp almond flour
- 1 tbsp unsweetened chocolate chips
- 1/4 tsp pumpkin pie spice
- 2 tbsp Swerve
- 1 tbsp pumpkin puree
- 1/2 cup mozzarella cheese, shredded

Directions:

1. Preheat your waffle maker.
2. In a small bowl, mix egg and pumpkin puree.
3. Add pumpkin pie spice, Swerve, almond flour, and cheese and mix well.
4. Stir in chocolate chips.
5. Spray waffle maker with cooking spray.
6. Pour half batter in the hot waffle maker and cook for 4 minutes. Repeat with the remaining batter.
7. Serve and enjoy.

Nutrition:

Calories 130

Fat 9.2 g

Carbohydrates 5.9 g

Sugar 0.6 g

Protein 6.6 g

Cholesterol 86 mg

Maple Chaffle

Preparation Time: 15 minutes
Servings: 2

Ingredients:

- 1 egg, lightly beaten
- 2 egg whites
- 1/2 tsp maple extract
- 2 tsp Swerve
- 1/2 tsp baking powder, gluten-free
- 2 tbsp almond milk
- 2 tbsp coconut flour

Directions:

1. Preheat your waffle maker.
2. In a bowl, whip egg whites until stiff peaks form.
3. Stir in maple extract, Swerve, baking powder, almond milk, coconut flour, and egg.
4. Spray waffle maker with cooking spray.
5. Pour half batter in the hot waffle maker and cook for 3-5 minutes or until golden brown. Repeat with the remaining batter.
6. Serve and enjoy.

Nutrition:

Calories 122
Fat 6.6 g
Carbohydrates 9 g

Sugar 1 g
Protein 7.7 g
Cholesterol 82 mg

Sweet Vanilla Chocolate Chaffle

Preparation Time: 10 minutes

Servings: 1

Ingredients:

- 1 egg, lightly beaten
- 1/4 tsp cinnamon
- 1/2 tsp vanilla
- 1 tbsp Swerve
- 2 tsp unsweetened cocoa powder
- 1 tbsp coconut flour
- 2 oz cream cheese, softened

Directions:

1. Add all ingredients into the small bowl and mix until well combined.
2. Spray waffle maker with cooking spray.
3. Pour batter in the hot waffle maker and cook until golden brown.
4. Serve and enjoy.

Nutrition:

Calories 312
Fat 25.4 g
Carbohydrates 11.5 g

Sugar 0.8 g
Protein 11.6 g
Cholesterol 226 mg

Choco Chip Lemon Chaffle

Preparation Time: 15 minutes

Servings: 2

Ingredients:

- 2 eggs, lightly beaten
- 1 tbsp unsweetened chocolate chips
- 2 tsp Swerve
- 1/2 tsp vanilla
- 1/2 tsp lemon extract
- 1/2 cup mozzarella cheese, shredded
- 2 tsp almond flour

Directions:

1. Preheat your waffle maker.
2. In a bowl, whisk eggs, Swerve, vanilla, lemon extract, cheese, and almond flour.
3. Add chocolate chips and stir well.
4. Spray waffle maker with cooking spray.
5. Pour 1/2 of the batter in the hot waffle maker and cook for 4-5 minutes or until golden brown. Repeat with the remaining batter.
6. Serve and enjoy.

Nutrition:

Calories 157

Fat 10.8 g

Carbohydrates 5.4 g

Sugar 0.7 g

Protein 9 g

Cholesterol 167 mg

Peanut Butter Sandwich Chaffle

Preparation Time: 15 minutes

Servings: 1

Ingredients:

For chaffle:

- 1 egg, lightly beaten
- 1/2 cup mozzarella cheese, shredded
- 1/4 tsp espresso powder
- 1 tbsp unsweetened chocolate chips
- 1 tbsp Swerve
- 2 tbsp unsweetened cocoa powder

For filling:

- 1 tbsp butter, softened
- 2 tbsp Swerve
- 3 tbsp creamy peanut butter

Directions:

1. Preheat your waffle maker.
2. In a bowl, whisk together egg, espresso powder, chocolate chips, Swerve, and cocoa powder.
3. Add mozzarella cheese and stir well.
4. Spray waffle maker with cooking spray.
5. Pour 1/2 of the batter in the hot waffle maker and cook for 3-4 minutes or until golden brown. Repeat with the remaining batter.
6. For filling: In a small bowl, stir together butter, Swerve, and peanut butter until smooth.
7. Once chaffles is cool, then spread filling mixture between two chaffle and place in the fridge for 10 minutes.
8. Cut chaffle sandwich in half and serve.

Nutrition:
Calories 190
Fat 16.1 g
Carbohydrates 9.6 g
Sugar 1.1 g
Protein 8.2 g
Cholesterol 101 mg

Cherry Chocolate Chaffle

Preparation Time: 10 minutes
Servings: 1

Ingredients:

- 1 egg, lightly beaten
- 1 tbsp unsweetened chocolate chips
- 2 tbsp sugar-free cherry pie filling
- 2 tbsp heavy whipping cream
- 1/2 cup mozzarella cheese, shredded
- 1/2 tsp baking powder, gluten-free
- 1 tbsp Swerve
- 1 tbsp unsweetened cocoa powder
- 1 tbsp almond flour

Directions:

1. Preheat the waffle maker.
2. In a bowl, whisk together egg, cheese, baking powder, Swerve, cocoa powder, and almond flour.
3. Spray waffle maker with cooking spray.
4. Pour batter in the hot waffle maker and cook until golden brown.
5. Top with cherry pie filling, heavy whipping cream, and chocolate chips and serve.

Nutrition:

Calories 264
Fat 22 g
Carbohydrates 8.5 g

Sugar 0.5 g
Protein 12.7 g
Cholesterol 212 mg

Expert

Bacon, Egg & Avocado Chaffle Sandwich
    Preparation Time: 5 minutes

    Cooking Time: 10 minutes

    Servings: 2

<u>Ingredients:</u>
- Cooking spray
- 4 slices bacon
- 2 eggs
- ½ avocado, mashed
- 4 basic chaffles
- 2 leaves lettuce

<u>Method:</u>
1. Coat your skillet with cooking spray.
2. Cook the bacon until golden and crisp.
3. Transfer into a paper towel lined plate.
4. Crack the eggs into the same pan and cook until firm.
5. Flip and cook until the yolk is set.
6. Spread the avocado on the chaffle.
7. Top with lettuce, egg and bacon.
8. Top with another chaffle.

<u>Nutritional Value:</u>
- Calories 372
- Total Fat 30.1g
- Saturated Fat 8.6g
- Cholesterol 205mg
- Sodium 943mg
- Total Carbohydrate 5.4g
- Dietary Fiber 3.4g
- Total Sugars 0.6g
- Protein 20.6g
- Potassium 524mg

Pumpkin Chaffles with Choco Chips

Preparation Time: 5 minutes

Cooking Time: 12 minutes

Servings: 3

Ingredients:

- 1 egg
- ½ cup shredded mozzarella cheese
- 4 teaspoons pureed pumpkin
- ¼ teaspoon pumpkin pie spice
- 2 tablespoons sweetener
- 1 tablespoon almond flour
- 4 teaspoons chocolate chips (sugar-free)

Method:

1. Turn your waffle maker on.
2. In a bowl, beat the egg and stir in the pureed pumpkin.
3. Mix well.
4. Add the rest of the ingredients one by one.
5. Pour 1/3 of the mixture to your waffle maker.
6. Cook for 4 minutes.
7. Repeat the same steps with the remaining mixture.

Nutritional Value:

- Calories 93
- Total Fat 7 g
- Saturated Fat 3 g
- Cholesterol 69 mg
- Sodium 138 mg
- Potassium 48 mg
- Total Carbohydrate 2 g
- Dietary Fiber 1 g
- Protein 7 g
- Total Sugars 1 g

Choco Waffle with Cream Cheese

Preparation Time: 5 minutes

Cooking Time: 8 minutes

Servings: 2

Ingredients:

Choco Chaffle

- 2 tablespoons cocoa powder
- 1 tablespoon almond flour
- ¼ teaspoon baking powder
- 2 tablespoons sweetener
- 1 egg, beaten
- ½ teaspoon vanilla extract
- 1 tablespoon heavy whipping cream

Frosting

- 2 tablespoons cream cheese
- 2 teaspoons confectioner's sugar (swerve)
- 1/8 teaspoon vanilla extract
- 1 teaspoon heavy cream

Method:

1. Combine all the choco chaffle ingredients in a large bowl, adding the wet ingredients last.
2. Mix well.
3. Plug in your waffle maker.
4. Pour half of the mixture into the device.
5. Close and cook for 4 minutes.
6. Cook the other waffle.
7. While waiting, make your frosting by adding cream cheese to a heat proof bowl.
8. Place in the microwave.
9. Microwave for 8 seconds.
10. Use a mixer to blend the cream cheese with the rest of the frosting ingredients.

11. Process until fluffy.

12. Spread the frosting on top of the chaffle.

13. Put another chaffle on top.

14. Pipe the rest of the frosting on top of the chaffle.

15. **Slice and serve.**

Nutritional Value:

- Calories 151
- Total Fat 13 g
- Saturated Fat 6 g
- Cholesterol 111 mg
- Sodium 83 mg
- Potassium 190 mg
- Total Carbohydrate 5 g
- Dietary Fiber 2 g
- Protein 6 g
- Total Sugars 1 g

Open-Faced Ham & Green Bell Pepper Chaffle Sandwich

Preparation Time: 10 minutes

Cooking Time: 10 minutes

Servings: 2

Ingredients:
- 2 slices ham
- Cooking spray
- 1 green bell pepper, sliced into strips
- 2 slices cheese
- 1 tablespoon black olives, pitted and sliced
- 2 basic chaffles

Method:
1. Cook the ham in a pan coated with oil over medium heat.
2. Next, cook the bell pepper.
3. Assemble the open-faced sandwich by topping each chaffle with ham and cheese, bell pepper and olives.
4. Toast in the oven until the cheese has melted a little.

Nutritional Value:
- Calories 365
- Total Fat 24.6g
- Saturated Fat 13.6g
- Cholesterol 91mg
- Sodium 1154mg
- Potassium 440mg
- Total Carbohydrate 8g
- Dietary Fiber 2.6g
- Protein 24.5g
- Total Sugars 6.3g

Sausage & Pepperoni Chaffle Sandwich

Preparation Time: 10 minutes

Cooking Time: 10 minutes

Servings: 4

Ingredients:

- Cooking spray
- 2 cervelat sausage, sliced into rounds
- 12 pieces pepperoni
- 6 mushroom slices
- 4 teaspoons mayonnaise
- 4 big white onion rings
- 4 basic chaffles

Method:

1. Spray your skillet with oil.
2. Place over medium heat.
3. Cook the sausage until brown on both sides.
4. Transfer on a plate.
5. Cook the pepperoni and mushrooms for 2 minutes.
6. Spread mayo on top of the chaffle.
7. Top with the sausage, pepperoni, mushrooms and onion rings.
8. Top with another chaffle.

Nutritional Value:

- Calories 373
- Total Fat 24.4g
- Saturated Fat 6g
- Cholesterol 27mg
- Sodium 717mg
- Potassium 105mg
- Total Carbohydrate 29.8g
- Dietary Fiber 1.1g
- Protein 8.1g
- Total Sugars 4.5g

Mini Keto Pizza

Preparation Time: 10 minutes

Cooking Time: 15 minutes

Servings: 2

Ingredients:

- 1 egg
- ½ cup mozzarella cheese, shredded
- ¼ teaspoon basil
- ¼ teaspoon garlic powder
- 1 tablespoon almond flour
- ½ teaspoon baking powder
- 2 tablespoons reduced-carb pasta sauce
- 2 tablespoons mozzarella cheese

Method:

1. Preheat your waffle maker.
2. In a bowl, beat the egg.
3. Stir in the ½ cup mozzarella cheese, basil, garlic powder, almond flour and baking powder.
4. Add half of the mixture to your waffle maker.
5. Cook for 4 minutes.
6. Transfer to a baking sheet.
7. Cook the second mini pizza.
8. While both pizzas are on the baking sheet, spread the pasta sauce on top.
9. Sprinkle the cheese on top.
10. Bake in the oven until the cheese has melted.

Nutritional Value:

- Calories 195
- Total Fat 14 g
- Saturated Fat 6 g
- Cholesterol 116 mg
- Sodium 301 mg
- Potassium 178 mg
- Total Carbohydrate 4 g
- Dietary Fiber 1 g
- Protein 13 g
- Total Sugars 1 g

Pumkpin Chaffle with Maple Syrup
Preparation Time: 5 minutes

Cooking Time: 16 minutes

Servings: 2

Ingredients:

- 2 eggs, beaten
- ½ cup mozzarella cheese, shredded
- 1 teaspoon coconut flour
- ¾ teaspoon baking powder
- ¾ teaspoon pumpkin pie spice
- 2 teaspoons pureed pumpkin
- 4 teaspoons heavy whipping cream
- ½ teaspoon vanilla
- Pinch salt
- 2 teaspoons maple syrup (sugar-free)

Method:

1. Turn your waffle maker on.
2. Mix all the ingredients except maple syrup in a large bowl.
3. Pour half of the batter into the waffle maker.
4. Close and cook for 4 minutes.
5. Transfer to a plate to cool for 2 minutes.
6. Repeat the steps with the remaining mixture.
7. Drizzle the maple syrup on top of the chaffles before serving.

Nutritional Value:
- Calories 201
- Total Fat 15 g
- Saturated Fat 8 g
- Cholesterol 200 mg
- Sodium 249 mg
- Potassium 271 mg
- Total Carbohydrate 4 g
- Dietary Fiber 1 g
- Protein 12 g
- Total Sugars 1 g

Swiss Bacon Chaffle

Preparation Time: 5 minutes

Cooking Time: 8 minutes

Servings: 2

Ingredients:

- 1 egg
- ½ cup Swiss cheese
- 2 tablespoons cooked crumbled bacon

Method:

1. Preheat your waffle maker.
2. Beat the egg in a bowl.
3. Stir in the cheese and bacon.
4. Pour half of the mixture into the device.
5. Close and cook for 4 minutes.
6. Cook the second chaffle using the same steps.

Nutritional Value:

- Calories 237
- Total Fat 17.6g
- Saturated Fat 8.1g
- Cholesterol 128mg
- Sodium 522mg
- Total Carbohydrate 1.9g
- Dietary Fiber 0g
- Total Sugars 0.5g
- Protein 17.1g
- Potassium 158mg

Bacon, Olives & Cheddar Chaffle

Preparation Time: 5 minutes

Cooking Time: 8 minutes

Servings: 2

Ingredients:

- 1 egg
- ½ cup cheddar cheese, shredded
- 1 tablespoon black olives, chopped
- 1 tablespoon bacon bits

Method:

1. Plug in your waffle maker.
2. In a bowl, beat the egg and stir in the cheese.
3. Add the black olives and bacon bits.
4. Mix well.
5. Add half of the mixture into the waffle maker.
6. Cover and cook for 4 minutes.
7. Open and transfer to a plate.
8. Let cool for 2 minutes.
9. Cook the other chaffle using the remaining batter.

Nutritional Value:

- Calories 202
- Total Fat 16g
- Saturated Fat 8g
- Cholesterol 122mg
- Sodium 462mg
- Potassium 111mg
- Total Carbohydrate 0.9g
- Dietary Fiber 0.1g
- Protein 13.4g
- Total Sugars 0.3g

Sausage & Egg Chaffle Sandwich

Preparation Time: 5 minutes

Cooking Time: 10 minutes

Serving: 1

Ingredients:

- 2 basics cooked chaffles
- 1 tablespoon olive oil
- 1 sausage, sliced into rounds
- 1 egg

Method:

1. Pour olive oil into your pan over medium heat.
2. Put it over medium heat.
3. Add the sausage and cook until brown on both sides.
4. Put the sausage rounds on top of one chaffle.
5. Cook the egg in the same pan without mixing.
6. Place on top of the sausage rounds.
7. Top with another chaffle.

Nutritional Value:

- Calories 332
- Total Fat 21.6g
- Saturated Fat 4.4g
- Cholesterol 139mg
- Potassium 168mg
- Sodium 463mg
- Total Carbohydrate 24.9g
- Dietary Fiber 0g
- Protein 10g
- Total Sugars 0.2g